#STAGNATIONMUSTFALL

100 PRACTICAL LESSONS
THAT WILL ACTIVATE
YOUR CAREER PROGRESSION

Publisher:
MindPower Publications
www.mindpowerpublications.com

Layout, Drawings & Cover Design: Elof Gribwagen

Copyright © 2015
by Siphiwe Moyo
www.siphiwemoyo.co.za

ISBN-13: 978-1519224415
ISBN-10: 1519224419

CONTENTS

INTRODUCTION

How it all started...

The day was 28 January 2014... It was 07:15am in the morning and I was a guest on a popular news and current affairs program, Morning Live on SABC 2. The interview was about Career Development or Career Progression, a subject matter I'm extremely passionate about.

The interviewer, Ms Leanne Manas asked me a question that went exactly like this "So Siphiwe, is career development a responsibility of an employer or an employee?" My answer was that career development is definitely the employee's responsibility and I added that the employer may create frameworks and guidelines, but each and every one of us are responsible for our own career progression.

As I was driving back after that interview, I thought to myself, "There are too many people who genuinely believe that their career advancement is in their employer's hands and they wonder why they don't get the bursaries or promotions they believe they deserve." It was at this point when the idea of writing this book was born.

In this book, I will present 100 lessons that will help you progress in your career. Some of these lessons will deal with the attitudes required to progress while some will be practical suggestions that you could use to advance your career and life immediately.

> *"I can't think of anything worse than living a stagnant life, devoid of change and improvement."*
> **John C. Maxwell**

1. UNDERSTAND THAT THINGS DON'T JUST HAPPEN

The day was Thursday the 4th of July 2002. It was 04:30 in the morning. It was dark. It was cold. I was standing at the Orange Farm train station, Stretford, waiting for the second Metrorail train of the day travelling from Vereeniging to Johannesburg, train number 9003 which was due to arrive at 04:44am. I was doing an Internship in Braamfontein at a company called Mining Qualifications Authority.

While waiting for the train, a friend of mine who was standing next to me says to me, "Siphiwe, this thing of waking up so early in the cold, rushing for a train, must stop; we must work hard, buy ourselves homes and cars and get out of this informal settlement." I was very inspired by the statement my friend proclaimed and was in complete agreement.

Many years later, I went back to Orange Farm and sadly found out that my friend was still travelling in the same Metrorail train number 9003 from Vereeniging to Johannesburg. I was very sad.

When I asked him what had happened to our dream of leaving Orange Farm for a better life, my friend said something that has actually made me write this book. He said, "Siphiwe, the system has blocked me from achieving that dream. The system has marginalised and ostracised us. The government that we have elected has neglected us. They eat alone and have forgotten about the people who voted for them. No one wants to give us tenders or even bursaries my friend. *Spijo* (this is what he called me), you're lucky that you managed to get out of this place."

I was shattered when I heard my friend utter those words. Look, I know that he was to a certain extent raising legitimate issues and I'm not at all trying to discredit his sentiments, but I believe his thinking was very erroneous because there are many other people who grew up in the same environment and similar circumstances yet still managed to rise above the obstacles and achieve greater things in life.

My friend therefore missed the plot in this regard, he needed to understand one of the most significant life lessons: knowing that **things don't just happen**. When

I convinced him that it is this mindset that is limiting his and many other people's progress, my friend gladly agreed that I refer to his story. I have thus set myself up on a mission to not only help my friend but also help all those who possess this limiting mentality by writing this book and sharing his story in this chapter. So if there's anything you ought to get out of this book, get this: if you're going to achieve progress in your career my friend, you have to understand this cruel fact: nothing just happens, we make things happen, intentionally so.

> *"Lives are not changed by intentions,*
> *but by actions."*
> **Brian Tracy**

2. DO NOT DESPISE SMALL BEGINNINGS

When I started studying for my first degree in 1999, I realised very soon that even though the National Student Financial Aid Scheme (NSFAS) was paying for my tuition, I still needed money for travelling to campus and other basic needs such as food. I then went to look for a job and fortunately got a part-time job at Mr Price clothing store in Southgate Mall, Johannesburg. I don't know what their wages are currently like but the casual employee's salary was very low then. I used to earn about R60. 00 per day yet still managed to maintain a very enthusiastic attitude in the three-year period I worked there.

There's someone I've been helping for a long time with some groceries and money, let's call him Jimmy. I recently decided to help Jimmy find a job and I did. Before completing the first month, Jimmy says to me that he wants to quit because, "I can't work for R150.00 per day," he said. Well, when I started working, I worked for three years earning R60.00 per day. It was in the year 1999 so assuming a 6% interest rate; this would be R152.45 per day today. So basically I worked three years for almost the same amount of money that 'Jimmy' can't work for. I know I can't force him to work but if he quits, he must never even think of calling me again for help.

I know you know people who have shared similar sentiments as Jimmy, I hope you do not partake in this nor possess this mindset because if you do, you still have a very long way to go in this life and career 'thing' my friend. We live in a society where people are only interested in the great end result and not the small beginnings. People want to be like you yet care less about what it took to get you where you are.

It appears that somehow people feel they are too big, too smart, special and powerful to start small. This 'go big or go home' discourse has become so predominant that it's ruining us. We are all too quick to celebrate significant achievements and not so much for the insignificant ones as they are not wrapped in gold and diamond packages.

Let me use this opportunity to highlight the paradox of hedonism or simply put, the paradox of happiness or pleasure from Positive Psychology. This phenomenon fundamentally states that ironically, we think the more we get what we want, in this instance pleasure, let's say from a promotion, the happier we will be when in fact, pursuing what we want (pleasure/promotion) becomes futile because we never get enough as long as that pleasure or happiness is external.

Think of it this way, when you're unemployed, your major concern is getting a job yet when you eventually get a junior position that pays you about R5, 000, you want R8, 000 and eventually that's also insufficient so you pursue R10, 000 and the list goes on. What a human condition we possess.

The key point I'm trying to make here is simple, in order to get to Point C, it makes logical sense to start in Point A and follow the steps. Therefore, if you want to earn R15, 000 then at some point, R5-8, 000 shouldn't be a *train smash*. It is therefore better and smarter to endure the lower amount for a certain period as it channels you to the desired amount than quitting because you are not getting what you want, when you want it.

As far as this matter is concerned, I believe all we really need is to grow up and stop acting like kids trapped in adult bodies. This whole 'instant gratification' phenomenon really needs to be buried by the time we reach adolescence. Instant gratification, starting big and getting what we feel we deserve is just not how life goes, well at least for the most part.

We all start somewhere so do not despise your small beginnings. It may appear small and insignificant but your latter end can still be greater. Indeed, you have potential to leave in utter shock those who think you are limited to where you are, above all, you have potential to completely shock yourself and be where you never thought you could be. It is possible and your small beginning should not be a disadvantageous factor, if anything, starting small should push you to want and pursue your big dreams relentlessly.

3. BE DISSATISFIED WITH YOUR CURRENT LEVEL

Some of my previous points may give an impression that I'm implying satisfaction with the small stuff. On the contrary though, we ought to be dissatisfied with the level we are currently at in order to get ahead. Rick Warren says, "The greatest enemy of tomorrow's success is today's success."

You have to be dissatisfied with your current role if you want to move. I used to take this for granted until I learned that some people don't actually want to move.

They don't aspire for more. They are simply okay doing what they are doing; and that's fine but if you want more, if you really want to move to the next level, you have to have a healthy level of discontentment because you can't move if you are satisfied.

To qualify my statement let me just say this, being dissatisfied is not the same as complaining, moaning, dreading your job and doing whatever it takes to show your bosses and colleagues how unhappy and miserable you are. For some reason, we tend to think this gives a loud and clear message to our managers but if anything, it actually makes very little room for advancement and improvement in our careers.

Therefore discontentment in this instance does not equate to any of these negative characteristics. Healthy levels of dissatisfaction thus imply a combination of negative and positive aspects of your current level that push you to aspire for more, with the negative dominated by the positive elements.

> "Something in human nature tempts us to stay where we are comfortable. We try to find a plateau, a resting place, where we have comfortable stress and adequate finances. Where we have comfortable associations with people, without the intimidation of meeting new people and entering strange situations." **Fred Smith**
>
> *"If what you did yesterday still looks big to you; you haven't done much today."*
> **Elbert Hubbard.**

4. MASTERING THE ART OF WANTING MORE AND STILL PERFORMING IN CURRENT ROLE

Some people tend to possess the 'happy in another life' mentality. You think you will be happier at your next job, with your next better boss and so in the meantime, you will just come to work to idle, chat, complain and call your bosses names while doing the bare minimal each day. Coming to work to show face and doing only what's necessary to ensure you don't get fired.

I'm not sure whether people do this because of logic or what but this is the quickest way to become stagnant. It's actually counterproductive if you think of it. I mean if you want to progress yet you not only possess but also strongly exhibit such attitudes and behaviours, how do you expect to get ahead. It's like doing the same thing over and over yet expecting different results, which will merely keep you exactly where you are.

I mean who wants to give a complainer a 'promo' and who wants to be led by a grumbler? Moreover, what evidence do you have to prove you will do better at your next job and be happier when you are clearly failing to keep yourself together in your current role? I have come to this conclusion: if you possess this unhealthy sense of dissatisfaction, I swear, nothing and I mean nothing, not even a salary increase will make your face glow, well at least not for long.

You see when you're unhappy and miserable, you have no reason to be grateful for anything and as a result, you get stuck in your sad little trapped cage. Not even a better job will rescue you because a few months down the line, you will most likely encounter similar challenges and characters. It's an attitude problem this, it's a matter of what's 'within' and not so much about what's on the outside. So in your dissatisfaction which I will now coin preparation for a better role or job altogether, remember to smile, give it your best shot and focus on the set target. In this way, you will find yourself in a better position to attract and receive the next great job.

5. LOOSE THE JOB DESCRIPTION MENTALITY

I have told you the story about my friend and I back in 2002 waiting for a train at 04:30am. Allow me to tell you a bit more detail of my engagements that year. As mentioned earlier, I was an intern at the Mining Qualifications Authority (MQA), which is a Sector Education & Training Authority (SETA) for the mining industry in South Africa. As far as I can remember, this was the first time the MQA hired interns and obviously, being an intern means you're the most low-ranking person in the organisation, which then implies that different people ask you to do all kinds of things.

One of the main tasks of the MQA was to organise skills development conferences in the mining sector. As interns (there were a few of us), we would be asked to assist with carrying boxes to and from the conference centres. We were however given a choice in this form of assistance, as it was not in our job description. Some of my fellow interns refused to do these tasks. They felt it was demeaning for them to do such menial tasks when they actually have Human Resource degrees. I also had a Human Resource degree but I chose to do it although it was outside my scope of work.

What my friends didn't' know was that when you help taking boxes to the conference centre and returning them back to the office you have to attend the conference by default. As an intern, I was therefore attending conferences and was exposed to discussions that were way ahead of my position.

In 2012, I was elected as Chairman of the South African Board for People Practices (SABPP), the professional body for Human Resource professionals in South Africa. Can you imagine what a shock this was to my friends? I can imagine how jaw dropping such unforeseen news must have been. I mean as far as I know, I'm the youngest ever Chairman of the SABPP.

I believe those discussions, which I was exposed to as an intern contributed to this. Sometimes, it's the so-called menial tasks that will activate your career progression. You may never know what may contribute to your upward mobility so forget the job description my friend; it will limit your progress.

6. GET RID OF FEAR

The reason many people don't progress is that they have fear. As Dostoevsky put it, "taking a new step, uttering a new word, is what most people fear most."

In order to move to the next level my friend, fear must fall. Fear inhibits progress. Don't be afraid of failure.

> *"The person interested in success has to learn to view failure as a healthy, inevitable part of the process of getting to the top."*
> **Dr Joyce Brothers**

In his book, The Psychology of Achievement, Brian Tracy writes about four millionaires who made their fortune by age thirty-five. They were involved in an average of seventeen businesses before finding the one that took them to the top. They kept on trying and changing until they found something that worked for them.

7. UNDERSTAND THAT SOMEONE IS ALWAYS WATCHING HOW YOU PERFORM THE SMALL TASKS

I'm a sought after professional speaker now but I can reassure you that it has not always been like that. In 2011, while I was still working for one of te big banks, I decided that I wanted a career in professional speaking and make it my means of income so before I resigned, I joined the Professional Speakers Association of Southern Africa (PSASA) as an associate member since I didn't qualify to be a professional member then.

One of the things I did after joining the PSASA was volunteering to do the tasks that most members didn't want to do: handling the registration desk, setting up before the meetings and packing things after our meetings. Ask anybody at the PSASA and they will tell you that these are the most dreaded tasks in the organisation. I continued doing these tasks for a while, faithfully so and to the best of my abilities even. Excellence is a practice after all. It was between 2013 and 2014 when I was surprisingly elected to be the Gauteng Chapter President of this amazing association and the person who had nominated me said the following: "We have watched how you did all the small tasks and therefore believe you can do the big tasks." This statement humbled me because it's a lesson I was taught as a young man, to be faithful in the little things.

The lesson in all this: whether you see them or not, whether you are aware of it or not, please know that someone is watching as you do those small tasks. Do yourself a favour and do them to the best of your ability. You may be working in obscurity, nobody may know your name and sometimes people might not even greet you, but be faithful in those tasks because someone is always watching.

8. UNDERSTAND THAT NOBODY OWES YOU A PROMOTION

Some people believe that their company owes them a promotion. Now, as I said, I am a Human Resource graduate and I know Labour Laws a bit and I can confirm this with you: nobody in your organisation owes you a promotion. So if you are going to get one, it will be because you work hard and nothing else.

It matters not how long you have been with your company, neither does it matter how much you have done for them, the clients you signed on board donkey years ago, whatever the case may be, whatever legitimate and valid reasons you may give to justify your entitlement, promotions are about current efforts and achievements and nothing besides hard work and going an extra mile is good enough to get you promoted.

9. PAY THE PRICE FOR PROGRESS

A story is often told about the famous Pablo Picasso. "One day a woman spotted him in the market and pulled out a piece of paper, "Mr. Picasso,' she said excitedly, 'I'm a big fan. Please, could you do a little drawing for me?" Picasso happily complied and quickly etched out a piece of art for her on the paper provided. He smiled as he handed it back to her and said, "That will be a million dollars. But Mr. Picasso" the flustered woman replied, "It only took you 30 seconds to do this little masterpiece. My good woman," Picasso laughed, "It took me 30 years to know how to do that masterpiece in 30 seconds."

There is absolutely no such a thing called instant success. There is no ready mix nor instant porridge when it comes to success, don't let the retailers fool you into this quick fix mindset.

The people that we celebrate now have been paying the price for a long time. We all have to pay the price to excel and succeed. Have a healthy work ethic, put in the hours, and commit yourself to your own learning, development and growth. Sacrifice the unnecessary outings, TV shows, social media and other idle time-wasting activities that steal your valuable and precious time. Now that is how you pay the price for progress.

> *"You can't have a million dollar dream and a minimum wage work ethic."*
>
> **Dr EMK Mathole**

10. THE PRINCIPLE OF FORWARD-LOOKING PREPARATION

I love listening to the radio during the holiday season because the main DJs/hosts are not there. In this period you are bound to discover some brilliant DJs/hosts who usually work in some strange hours of the morning. This is how I always see and think of it: whatever opportunity you want, the main person is bound to go on holiday, get sick or something of the sort. The question is not whether that day will come but whether you will be ready when that opportunity comes?

John Maxwell puts it this way, "When opportunity comes, it's too late to prepare." Read up on most artists and how they were discovered, despite auditions that are prepared for with much work and effort, there are also beautiful stories of 'random selections', which we know are not so random. If you want to be a manager at some point, exhibit your management qualities and style before the role is given to you.

I strongly advise everyone, intern or manager to read 'Leading without a Title' by Robin Sharma and thank me later. That book fundamentally teaches one of the most significant lessons in life; that you do not need to be what you want to be to start acting like it, in fact, you can act like it before you become it so that by the time you officially become it, the process and adjustments are seamless. You see leadership is a state of mind not a state of position.

Set your mind right and position it into leadership first before you need to act and live it out and the challenges will be easily surmountable. This applies to all sorts of things we want in life. It may sound overrated but how you think and what you set and engage your brilliant mind upon to determine whom you become and what you possess. As they often say: you are what you think. Even now, wherever you are, if you feel lost and unsure how to reach your destination, simply trace your thoughts and you will get your answer.

Likewise, if you want to change your position and state of affairs, start in your mastermind. It's really that simple and never too late my friend, there is absolutely nothing the mind can fail at despite what we limit it to and the boundaries we set through our thoughts. Don't be the reason for your stagnancy, deliberately channel yourself and set yourself up for success in the top-down fashion, from the mind to your actions and eventually habits.

11. UNDERSTAND THAT YOU CAN'T PROGRESS IN YOUR LIFE AND CAREER WITHOUT SACRIFICE, YOU JUST CAN'T

It is normal for entrepreneurs to downgrade or even sell their cars to start a business. The logic is simple really; if you can't even downgrade your car to follow your dream, then you simply don't want it enough. Many people have had to sacrifice far more than a car downgrade.

Strive Masiyiwa, telecoms billionaire tells a fascinating story about how he financed his business. He started his business journey in 1986 with just US$75, going around suburbs fixing broken lights and gates. After running the business for a while, he needed additional funding so he went to a Barclays' bank branch seeking a loan.

He drove his car, parked it outside the bank and went in to pitch to the banker. "After listening to my pitch, she asked, "Is that your car?" To which he replied yes and she then said, "Go sell it and I will match whatever it is you sell it for, that is my way of knowing whether you are serious or not." "So I took my car away... I sold it and I came back the following day. I had the money in cash, I put it on her table and I said: "Where is yours?" And I haven't looked back ever since." He said.

> *"Dreams do come true, if only we wish hard enough. You can have anything in life if you will sacrifice everything else for it."*
> **J.M. Barrie, Peter Pan**

Sacrifice is a prerequisite to success. As the most famous sacrifice quote says, "If you don't sacrifice for what you want then what you want will be the sacrifice." Be willing to loose something for a greater gain, sacrifice!

12. PEOPLE WHO ARE TOO NICE TO YOU WILL LIMIT YOUR CAREER PROGRESS

When I was working at the MQA, the Chief Executive Officer was the late Dr Menzi Mthwecu. When my boss started being comfortable with my work, she said I could submit my work directly to him. Every time I submitted something to him, he would print it, and then use his red pen to make all kinds of corrections, in what would seem to be an extremely rude manner. In addition to this, he would often tell me how I've wasted his time by submitting such 'nonsense' to him.

For a while I thought he really hated me until one day, he called me into his office and said to me, "You know why I'm very hard on you?" I was standing there thinking, "Oh, he actually knows he's hard on me." He continued to say; "I'm hard on you because I think you have potential. If I didn't think so, I would not waste my time on you. I would just ask Chernice (my direct manager) to stop allowing you to deal directly with me. I think you're going to be a leader in the skills development arena."

The bottom line in this story is this; a manager who understands too much when you are producing sloppy work actually thinks you're not worth their time to correct you. Managers invest in potential so if you feel your manager is pushing you towards your limits and overworking you, instead of complaining and grumbling, thank them and allow yourself to fully utilise, explore and exploit your potential. Aim to excel and accept constructive criticism with humility and a smile on your face, knowing that you are worth their time.

13. EXPOSURE PROPELS PROGRESS

Some people are no longer progressing in their careers because they spend too much time with people who admire them. They strongly possess a 'mama I made it' mentality yet they are so much further than they think. Thoughts and statements such as "I'm the man" "I'm the only one with a degree in my family" "I have been the first in getting the best things in life within my network" and all such things are seriously hampering their progress.

I remember in 2009 when I also began showing symptoms of this type of mind-set. You see I had already left Orange Farm, staying in some middle class suburb and every time I went home on weekends, the people in Orange Farm used to tell me how much I inspire them and so on. This happened for a long time, until one evening, I was going to a meeting in a place called Atholl in Sandton. It was one of those meetings held in someone's house. I still remember my arrival as though it was yesterday, they opened a gate for me and the first thing I saw in the yard was a tennis court. I couldn't believe I'm seeing a tennis court in someone's backyard. I remember asking my fellow traveller, "Dude, is this like the community tennis court?" My friend just said "Siphiwe, please don't embarrass me!"

When we finally got to the house, we were escorted to one of the rooms; I'm not sure what it's called. Please accommodate me here, remember that black people in South Africa still refer to a lounge as a dining room. So taking this into consideration, there I was, in a house with four different rooms that all had couches. I'm not sure what to call them. I'm not sure whether I should sit, kneel, and lift my hands in worship or what? That's when I had an awakening. It hit me that day that I was not as successful as I thought I was; that I was not as successful as my friends in Orange Farm thought I was. I had not made it yet!

At that point, my dream changed. I had seen better; I had seen something to aspire to. I know that was a very material thing but for me this was a lesson nothing else had taught me. I learned a valuable lesson that day; I learnt that exposure does change your dreams and ambitions; it changes your definition of success. If you are no longer hungry for more, check what you are exposed to. It is possible that maybe you are hanging around people who adore you too much.

There is such a strong power we seem to dismiss in the workplace, the power of associations. You see, if you hang around the complainers, gossipers and lazy bones, you may not be one of them yet but sooner or later you most likely will, slowly but surely. Likewise, if you want to be evaluated on a positive light, hang around with the optimists, the hard workers and bosses' favourites, it will put you in a very good place.

14. DON'T OVERPLAY THE ROLE OF NETWORKING AND RELATIONSHIPS; YOU STILL NEED TO PERFORM

"It's not about what you know, it's about who you know." Fair enough, but I personally think this statement is ridiculously overplayed. Unfortunately it's not all that plain and simple, what you know is actually very important to progress in your career as well. Many South Africans who get jobs in the corporate sector actually didn't know anyone in those organisations. In fact, most of the jobs I've ever had in my career are jobs I got because I applied through normal channels and my application met the necessary requirements and thus became successful.

I say most because obviously in internal company positions, people get to know you and what you can do, which is a different matter altogether. I do agree that relationships and networks are important to get ahead but I think we tend to exaggerate the role they play in career progression. I mean even if someone puts through your CV, your CV still needs to look good and you still need to impress in the interview. Most significantly though, once you are offered that job, you must deliver. So be not deceived because what you know is still very important to get ahead.

So in summary, relate well with people, network, make contacts and maintain positive relationships but above all, know your job and do it well too.

15. YOUR BOSS DOES HAVE FAVOURITES; THEY ARE CALLED GOOD PERFORMERS. WANT TO BE ONE? PERFORM

As someone who worked in Human Resource Development for a long time, one of the complaints we often dealt with was this, "Our boss only listens to her blue-eyed boy and no-one else." In fact, to be honest, I have uttered those statements myself. At that point, it seemed to me and many others that a manager just decides to favour one person over others, until I observed something... I had an awakening, another 'aha' moment upon the realisation that almost all the bosses' favourites were exceptional performers.

There may be one crazy manager who has favourites based on another criteria but in the main, it is because that employee works extremely hard and continually makes their manager look good. Try it and thank me later.

16. UNDERSTAND THAT YOUR BOSS WILL TAKE CREDIT FOR YOUR WORK; THAT'S JUST HOW IT WORKS

Many people don't get this; they often come to us and complain about their managers taking credit for their work. They would whisper things like, "You know I actually created that strategy and all he did was present it, and now he's acting like it was all his idea." Well in case you didn't know, let me brief you about your manager's role — the job of a manager is to get results through other people. You should therefore be very happy and pleased if your manager presents your work as it is because it shows the confidence they have in you.

Can we please stop complaining about the petty inevitable things? Managers don't fundamentally exist to create and come up with the work; they fundamentally exist to facilitate it. The sooner you accept this, the happier you will be in your career journey.

17. NEVER TRY TO OUTSHINE YOUR BOSS – YOU WON'T WIN

Many years ago, I read a book titled 'The 48 Laws of Power' by Robert Greene and the very first lesson you find there is to never outshine your master. Contrary to popular belief, all of us have a responsibility to ensure that those above us feel comfortably superior. You should therefore do everything possible to make sure that your boss does not see you as someone trying to be smarter than him – trust me, it is a bad idea and you will live to regret it.

In your defence though, I understand how it may be difficult to carry out such duties as some managers make it hard to and thus you may easily opt to outshine him. Your colleagues may cheer you for this but please bear in mind that in the end, whether you're outshining your boss out of spite, because they deserve it or any other reason will essentially do more harm to you than good. Ask anyone who has attempted this or any other attempts to paint a negative picture of their boss and they will tell you, whether they were right or wrong, it just never ends well my friend. Therefore, never set yourself on this doomed mission, as it will only explode on your face and not your bosses'.

18. CONTRARY TO POPULAR BELIEF, YOUR BOSS AND YOUR SENIOR LEADERSHIP ACTUALLY WANT YES MEN/WOMEN IN THEIR TEAM

I think many people engage in a lot of self-deception by saying things like, "My boss does not want a yes-man/woman, he wants us to challenge him." Really? Let me be straight on this one: every boss wants team members who say yes more than they say no. Nobody wants a 'Mmusi Maimane' in their team. For those who don't know, Mmusi Maimane is the parliamentary leader of the official opposition party in South Africa, Democratic Alliance (DA).

People need to understand that a person like Mmusi is actually paid to oppose, you on the other hand are not. I'm not suggesting you say yes all the time but I guarantee you, saying yes more than you say no will work out to your advantage.

19. YOU MUST EARN THE RIGHT TO DIFFER WITH YOUR BOSS. IF YOU ARE NOT AN EXCEPTIONAL PERFORMER, YOU MUST KEEP QUIET AND DO AS YOU'RE TOLD

If you are not fully functioning in your role, you must keep quiet and do what you are told to do. Sometimes you find people who are not even performers thinking they can just challenge their bosses. Do your job first, and then you will earn your boss's ear regarding a different way of doing things. You can't be entitled to an opinion when you have not earned that right. Prove yourself worthy of the position and you will be worth hearing and your points regarded as noteworthy. Until then, your lack of performance and reputation as a low or average performer will always serve as a hindrance.

20. IF YOU AND YOUR BOSS HAVE A DIFFERENT OPINION ON HOW SOMETHING SHOULD BE DONE, DO IT THE WAY YOUR BOSS WANTS IT. YOU ARE NOT THE BOSS!

Once upon a time, I used to have a colleague who used to have unnecessary arguments with our boss. She would insist that the template in which the boss wanted her reports did not make sense. She argued that there was a better way of submitting those reports and she was quite vocal about it.

Here's a noteworthy fact: in the workplace, things such as report templates are merely a matter of preference and unfortunately as an employee; you have no authority to determine how they should be done. Your preference can therefore not be adhered to because you are not the boss, so kindly spare us the drama and submit them the way your boss prefers and wants them. If you keep arguing with your boss about such things, you create unnecessary tension between the two of you and that will hamper your career progress.

Look, I'm not saying you should never disagree with your boss, but some things are just a matter of preference so just submit. Unfortunately it's one of those 'because I said so' kinds of situations. If you and your boss have a different opinion on how something should be done, simply do it the way your boss wants it and withdraw your case. It's that simple really, you don't have to agree with it, you just have to do it regardless.

21. DON'T BE A HIGH MAINTENANCE EMPLOYEE; YOU ARE THERE TO MAKE LIFE EASIER FOR YOUR BOSSES, NOT MORE DIFFICULT

There is no manager who wants to have a high maintenance employee. A high maintenance employee is a person who is way too needy, more like a child trapped in an adult's body. They moan, they groan, they want special attention and special treatment literally all the time. Some people are always taking leave for this and that and they have all kinds of favours to ask for. They have all sorts of things they expect their managers and colleagues to understand. They have enough problems and work can't add onto their stress.

Allow me to let you in on a little secret, for those of you who have never worked in HR, please allow me to tell you that if you are abusing sick leave, your manager knows. If you get sick every time you have to make a decision, how do you expect to be given a position where you will have to make decisions every hour? You will never be considered for any form of promotion if you keep going like that. You will do all that you do and have always done for decades, same chair, same desk, same tasks and all. Your working days will appear like a movie on replay, no new challenge, no new role.

Let me add this, if you are high maintenance, you are easily disposable. I mean why should your employer hold onto you when you give them no reason to? If anything, you keep proving how expensive you are and what a loss and waste of the company's resources and benefits you are. You see the basic 'tit for tat' rule always applies, even at work. Don't be high maintenance my friend; it will hamper your chances of progression. You are actually employed to make your manager's life easier not more difficult. Stop with the excuses now and rebuild your reputation.

22. THE 'OPEN DOOR POLICY' DOES NOT MEAN THE DOOR IS OPEN ALL THE TIME

Many organisations have open plan offices these days, which is becoming a problem as some employees fail to understand this simple phenomenon: the fact that your manager is at her desk does not mean she is available for you. Let me break the news; having an employee who constantly comes to your desk unannounced is disturbing and awfully irritating. If you want to meet, I know for a fact that most things are never that urgent so if the building is not burning and the client is not threatening to switch agencies then it can wait.

If you don't want to be a nuisance to your boss, here's my advice: learn to write a list of all you need clarity on and get all your stories and points straight, then you can schedule a 15 to 30-minutes session or meeting with your manager as an appropriate platform to have a discussion with her. The point here is to only go to your manager's desk when necessary.

23. ALWAYS MAKE YOUR BOSS LOOK GOOD – ALWAYS

If you want to get ahead in your career, it means someday you want to be someone's boss as well. The principle here is simple, apply the Golden Rule: do unto others, as you would like them to do unto you. Treat your boss as you would want your subordinates to treat you; in how you address and represent them, in your attitude, work ethic and basic human courtesy.

Do not dehumanise your boss into a monster whether they deserve it or not, that will hinder you from treating them with respect and having a good working relationship with them, which will in turn block your progress. Imagine the effort it takes to be mean and spiteful to your boss, is not easier to make them look good instead? Speak highly of them, let them take the credit; let them shine on your spotlight, that's why he or she is the boss and that's why you will be soon.

24. TAKE INITIATIVE

> *"One of the fastest ways to put your career onto the fast track, to become more valuable, is to develop and maintain the power of initiative."*
>
> **Brian Tracy**

Nothing seriously says 'you got this' like taking the right initiative in your work. I say right initiative because unfortunately there is such a thing as wrong initiative, which can do far more harm than good to your career.

For example, if your manager is not around to make a certain call and you make a wrong or uninformed decision or you make what appears to be a right and smart decision to you only to have it bite you later on because it wasn't so right after all.

Unfortunately most of us are so concerned with proving our ability to take initiative that sometimes we cut corners and apply certain measures that do not comply with our industry or company systems, processes and even policies. Taking the right initiative requires a thorough assessment of the case and implementation of proven methods. You don't have to invent to prove you can take initiative, you can do what your manager would do and maybe do it better, smarter and efficiently.

However, sometimes one does need to take risks as I mentioned and the truth is that very few things offer you the ability to take risks in the work environment as the opportunity to take initiative would. In such a case, ensure that whatever you are about to do will not come back to bite you, employ all the necessary measures and ensure your innovative strategy has been tested to effectively solve the issue at hand.

I think I have made the significant point I wanted to make in this chapter but I will rephrase it nonetheless. Taking initiative is necessary for your career growth; it shows you can manage your work and that you can think out of the box. It shows you can handle responsibility and ensure successful completion of your tasks. Taking initiative will definitely build your reputation as innovative, creative and hardworking, which will absolutely score you some great points and enhance your chances of career advancement and promotion.

However, taking initiative also comes with the responsibility to adhere to systems and processes. Moreover, it requires confidence in your implementation and depending on the risks involved, guaranteed success of your ideas or methods in order to work for, instead of against you.

Please remember that sometimes when you are required to take initiative it may be on smaller tasks and therefore thinking on your feet is required. In such times, elements such as innovation and creativity may not necessarily come into play and that's okay because sometimes it's really just about making a seemingly obvious decision or presenting a simple idea. The point is to ensure that whatever you suggest or implement is relevant and effective for your project and that it will be fruitful and produce the desired outcome.

25. SOMETIMES YOU WILL FEEL GOOSE BUMPS WHEN YOU WORK AND SOMETIMES YOU WON'T. IT'S CALLED WORK FOR A REASON. JUST DO IT!

Producing sloppy work that lacks creativity and passion as a result of your lack of inspiration and interest is plain immaturity. Remember how in school, you had to pass a module whether you liked and enjoyed it or not? Remember how whether the lecturer was boring or exciting made no difference to the fact that you still needed to produce good work in order to receive good marks? Well, the principle remains the same. Whether you like your job or not, whether you like doing some aspects of your job over others makes no difference, you still have to do it and you have to do it all and do it well.

Work is not nursery school, your manager is not there to beg you to do your job nor nurse your feelings and be your motivational speaker. That's your job and nobody else's. A workplace is not a university; you don't choose and decide what you want to do and when you'll do it. If you have to do paperwork despite your great personality and passion for working with people over machines, you just have to stick it out and do it. No job is perfect and rosy; every job has both its perks and quirks.

It's very important to know that when it comes to your job, it's not just about the output but attitude, especially when you have to do the not so favourite parts of your role. Simply put, how you do your job, i.e. your attitude towards your job really says a lot about you. Refuse to allow your preferences to hinder and destroy your professional reputation. No company and absolutely no manager wants to work with a person who will only do great work when they feel like it and not so great because they lack passion for other aspects of their job. The truth about work is that often, you have to work even when you have zero inspiration. Only immature people wait for inspiration before they work. Imagine if we only worked when we felt like it? That may be never for some, in fact, it would be a disaster to rely on feelings to do our jobs. Often, we have to tell our body: shut up and work in order to get things done.

26. YOU MUST BE WILLING TO TRAVEL OR RELOCATE. THE JOB OF YOUR DREAMS MIGHT NOT BE IN JOHANNESBURG, CAPE TOWN OR DURBAN

One day, I saw a CV of a 20 year old that said she was not willing to relocate from Johannesburg. Now, maybe there were valid reasons for her reluctance to travel such as a sick parent or maybe she was taking care of her siblings, but generally speaking or rather writing, no 20 year old should say that on their CV. It is very limiting. Why are we limiting ourselves so much?

As older people and members of the society in general, we have to be careful what we say to these young souls. While we're on that, can we please stop telling 22 year-old girls "God is going to give you a husband?" Give you a husband for what? How about, "Have you applied for that scholarship to Oxford, Harvard or Insead?" Or "Did you hear about the R100 billion that the IDC has put aside to fund value-adding businesses?"

Back to my initial point, I was recently presenting a keynote address at the University of Limpopo and during several discussions with other people in the area, I had an 'aha' moment, a real awakening: there are serious business opportunities outside of Gauteng, I must stop obsessing over Gauteng. So I had to learn this as well. Your destiny and career is not tied to where you are currently located, be willing to move.

27. RECIPROCAL/MUTUAL SUPPORT

One of the key problems we have in our country is that of entitlement. Moreover, one of the biggest signs that you possess this exaggerated sense of self-worth/pride is when you expect others to support your hustle when you never support them, that is, if you preach but never allow yourself to be preached to. If you speak at conferences but you are never a delegate. If you expect colleagues to help you at work but you never help anyone. If you organize concerts but never attend other people's shows.

It's amazing how some people expect others to give that which they fail to, I mean just drop your 'prima donna' attitude and give that which you expect. When people come through for you, you have no idea what it takes and what they sacrifice to show up and support you, the least you can do is return the favour, whether they expect it or not. Indeed, we are aware of those of you who will only come through because you feel you owe us one, which lacks sincerity because nothing is more genuine and fulfilling than one who supports you simply because they can and want to. This is really just basic human courtesy; adopting such mannerisms seriously does no harm.

So my advice, if a colleague is stuck and you know you can help, if you have to go an extra mile now and again just to help the other, if you can sacrifice (within limits of course) for the sake and benefit of the other, then by all means do. You see in the work environment, there are very subtle and unwritten human relation rules. These rules are unspoken yet they have so much impact on how others treat you. You may not know it but some of the reasons you may feel the world is against you at work may be because you gave people reasons to be against you.

You don't have to be a people pleaser and a yes man/woman but simple acts of kindness and support to your colleagues will surely take you a long way. Remember the saying, 'you may forget how you treat people but they will not forget how you treat them?' Well, its' true so watch it. Being nice costs nothing but a smile, a helping hand and an extra mile here and there and giving it when they least neither expect nor demand it is totally priceless.

For those of you who take pride in being the mean boss, lighten up and let your hair loose a bit. Be friendly and do your best to give what you can because no man is an island and someday, you will need the same or similar help. It's not that they keep a record no, it's that everything you do counts for or against you. Yes, those people keep tabs, just as you do. So the sooner you accept that you are not an exception to the rule, the better your relations.

28. BE NICE TO PEOPLE, BE HELPFUL TO COLLEAGUES – TRUST ME YOU WILL NEED THEM

Every person you meet is a potential door to a new opportunity, this is the kind of attitude we should possess when we meet, relate and deal with people. I'm not saying we must reduce humanity to mere windows of opportunity but because we can easily forget the impact others may have on us, whether now or in the future. It's therefore necessary to adopt this mindset.

You never know what that cleaner may be in the future, you never know what your subordinate is capable of and sometimes life will force you to need the people you think you may never need. So remember to be nice and helpful even to those who don't deserve it, that kindness will go a long way. The point is to relate with everyone in such a manner that when such a time comes, because trust me it always does, you can easily humble yourself and ask for help instead of requesting it shamefully and regrettably.

Be nice, usually all it takes is a smile, a greeting, a sweet response, priceless acts of kindness and minor sacrifices from you. Sometimes our destinies are indeed tied to others and the truth is, the person you are terribly mean to may only unlock your opportunities. You might not know it because maybe at this point, you are on top and they are at the bottom of the food chain. However, I think at this age and point in time, we are all aware of how easily and quickly the wheel may turn and things may change, so remember to be nice in all your dealings and relations with people my friend.

29. BUILD YOUR REPUTATION

Your reputation is one of the most significant elements that determine how people treat and relate to you. Interestingly though, reputation development is a slow process as it takes time to build and the building never really gets complete due to the continuous alterations.

I want you to realise in this chapter that you make or break yourself depending on the reputation you have built in the workplace. Ironically, we tend to think our reputations are beyond our control when they are consciously formed, developed and transformed. Ever wondered why Peter could be known as a sweet somebody yet you know him as a harsh person? I bet you it's because your encounters with him have been quite harsh and thus it sounds crazy to you that Peter can be a sweetheart.

You see the error in our human condition is the assumption that subtle things such as these are beyond us and we erroneously leave it to others and external factors. Furthermore, the discourse of 'people see what they want to see' has not helped us much in this regard. My point here is this; whether you are aware of it or not, it's up to you which tasks you are given and trusted with at work and why they are given and trusted to you. Therefore, if you have made it as the office player, the lazy bone, and the complainer or on a more positive light, the hard worker, it has all been by choice, consciously or unconsciously so.

The sooner you realise and accept this, the better position you are in to reclaim your authority, reshape and redesign your reputation. In a work environment, it's therefore significant to be known as dependable, professional and cooperative. It always amazes me how certain people just don't get this. You acquire a reputation in your daily actions, outputs, behaviours, words and attitudes. Be mindful of how you portray yourself in this regard, it may just make or break you.

30. AVOID THE 'WE'VE ALWAYS DONE IT LIKE THIS' BRIGADE

In all organisations, there are those people I call the 'we've always done it like this brigade.' These are the people who have been there forever, literally. Nothing moves nor shakes them, nothing surprises them and absolutely nothing inspires them anymore. They could not be bothered by any of it, neither change nor innovation, even change management solutions don't work on them. They think they know everything to such an extent that they wouldn't know a creative idea even if it were presented to them on a silver platter.

Again we go back to the power of associations. These people will suck every ounce of energy from you; they will demotivate and literally kill your enthusiasm, optimism and ambitions at work. There's only one solution in dealing with them: avoid them at all costs!

31. NEVER HIDE BEHIND AN EMAIL ADDRESS. NO ONE PROMOTES AN ANONYMOUS PERSON!

One day, I was talking to a Human Resource Consultant in a company of about 250 people. He mentioned to me that because they are a multinational company and highly advanced in technology, often people literally start working in that organisation without him knowing about it. The person's potential boss might be sitting in Dubai and therefore interviews are conducted through web-based tools. After confirming that the employee will be employed, he/she receives an employment contract and other on-boarding documents online. They then have to sign and upload them and someone based in India receives them (you know how India is with outsourcing).

The orientation process kicks in before the employee starts. She gets links to choose benefits and beneficiaries and regularly gets SMSes giving him directions, direct manager details and all such information before the start day. Because of the nature of this business, he often finds out after a week or so that the new employee has started.

In organisations such as these, it is possible to burry yourself in your work and go about your business day in and day out, keeping to yourself. Whether it's by choice or circumstances, you can easily find that people don't actually know you beyond your email address. My friend, don't be tempted to be 'an email address.' You are so much more than your name @ a company dot com. Dare to be visible and don't let the anonymity fool you because you have to be known in order to be pushed, recommended and advanced in your career.

32. WIDTH WITHOUT DEPTH WILL LIMIT YOUR CAREER PROGRESSION

In order to grow in your career, you need both career width and depth. In this context, width refers to having varied experience from different disciplines and divisions, whereas depth refers to being an expert in what you do. I studied for both an MBA and an Executive Development Program. These are both general management qualifications and thus intended to give me width. These programmes offer a very superficial understanding of literally everything that happens in an organisation and are therefore excellent for this purpose.

However, I'm also a human resources/learning professional, and in my profession and most probably yours as well, it's very important that I acquire depth. One of the reasons we lack a skilled workmanship is because many people don't stay long enough in a position to acquire the necessary depth. People work for a few months, a year or two and want out, they move on too quickly.

Don't get me twisted, I know I said people shouldn't stay in one organisation forever but it is important not to leave too early either – it's a balancing act this thing comrade. This is where it's important to practice the law of equilibrium and, as Aristotle would say, the art of moderation. Moderation is key in your career my friend, whether you are sought after or you have proven yourself is not the point, the point is knowing when to leave and when to stay.

I think we all know to learn and master anything in life requires consistent effort and practice. Read up on the one thousand hours theory, apparently to excel in anything and achieve mastery, you must have done that particular thing for about a thousand hours, do the math and count how many days that is and you will know how long it takes to master anything.

I think my point has been made thus far. You have to stay on that job to master it. That is why it's important to determine earlier on which career path you want to follow. I know it can be a long, daunting and confusing process but the sooner you figure it out the better. Don't be the man or woman who discovers their path on their 15th job, in their 10th company within 20 years. Commit yourself to choosing your path, learning and empowering yourself in it and eventually excelling there.

33. TAKING OFFENSE EASILY WILL HINDER YOUR CAREER PROGRESSION

Have you ever worked with people who are so fragile that you are even afraid of giving them feedback?

People need to toughen up a bit, I tell you. Senior people in you organisation will offend you, guaranteed.

The relationship between offense and your career is generally linear. Offense leads to career regression, you will not go any further if people need to watch how and what they say to you. If you can't take criticism, whether it's destructive or constructive is not the point, you just have to take it and deal with it. Moreover, you not only have to take it but you must receive it without an attitude or a dramatic verbal or non-verbal response.

You see, being tough in this regard will always work to your advantage because if you're toughened up and not a cry-baby, there's a maturity and seriousness about you. There's a courage and wisdom portrayed and associated with you. You build a reputation and give a strong message about your character, that you cannot only take it but you can handle it. Be known as that person and if it really cuts deep, because certain things have that power, then handle it on your own, keep it to yourself or among your family and close friends.

34. UNDERSTAND THAT WORK IS AN ENDLESS INTERVIEW

Yes I said it; each and every day you spend at work is a continuous interview. Let me get this straight: you can arrive in the office as late as you can get away with, take the longest lunches, do as little as possible, leave as early as possible but when you are being interviewed for a senior position in the organisation, you want to pull the "I'm willing to push beyond boundaries" card? What boundaries are you pushing beyond?

You may think nobody is watching nor paying attention but trust me, someone is, people are always watching you, every day and every moment. Consider yourself as having a stalker, watch your back, and watch your words and actions. Above all, watch your professional etiquette and mannerisms. Understand that you are in an interview all day, every day. It is forever on-going and never ending.

The great thing about this interview though is that because of its endless nature, you have an opportunity to improve and change your responses every day. You know how after an interview, you think of all the great and amazing responses you should have given but they were just not in the tip of your tongue? Well this interview is so great; you can give your best response the next day and better yet, the next hour if you are not impressed with yourself.

The danger though, is that because this interview is never ending, one can easily get comfortable and thus fail to see the area they are not doing great in and therefore need to improve or work on. With this chapter, I hope you have a daily reminder and consciousness of the interview without an exit door.

35. DON'T GIVE UP ON YOUR DREAM

Sometimes giving up may seem like the easiest thing to do but you need to know this: if you're going to progress, you need to strongly possess the 'no quit zone' in your mind, the type of mentality that says giving up is not an option! The only justifiable reasons for quitting should only be if it's the wisest, rightest and best thing to do, not because it's an option and certainly not because it's the easiest and least effortful way out.

I know life can really get hard sometimes, it can knock and push you way beyond what you think you can handle. Believe me when I say there have been days when giving up seemed to be the way to go and I'm certain that most of us have reached that point. The point in which things are just not coming together and our dreams feel too far-fetched and unrealistic. Sadly, a lot of people allow circumstances and these difficulties to convince them that they will never reach their goals. Moreover, they are further convinced that the earlier they give in, the better off they are, as it would save them from hustles and embarrassments.

As I was finalizing this book, South African local hip hop artist, Cassper Nyovest, reached one of his dreams to become the first in SA to fill the 20 000 seating capacity in Northgate, Johannesburg, without an assistance of an international act. What a moment that was. What is your dream?

A few years ago, I was attending a conference for people in the events industry and someone on stage said this, "Every day, there are about 300 conferences in SA." I was so frustrated by that statement as I thought to myself, "If there are 300 conferences each day in the country, then why am I speaking once in 2 months?" My speaking engagements have become more frequent now, I'm not where I should be but I'm definitely not where I was a few years ago either and that's because I didn't give up on my dream.

I strongly believe that if you can't go through a day without thinking about it, giving up is absolutely not an option. It must mean that much to you to pursue it without restraint and giving in. Can you imagine where technology would be if Steve Jobs quit? Where the Virgin Group would be if Richard Branson quit, would it even exist? No! Moreover, have you imagined where South Africa would be if the likes of Steve Biko, the 1976 youth, Nelson Mandela and Walter Sisulu quit? The key point here is that all these great and life-changing achievements, trends and icons we now identify as successful were not birthed without struggle and temptations to quit.

36. NOBODY WILL EVER CARE ABOUT YOUR DEVELOPMENT MORE THAN YOU. IF YOU LEAVE IT INTO SOMEONE ELSE'S HANDS, IT WON'T HAPPEN

Here's an interesting workplace fact: managers do care a bit about your development but they care more about performance. If you really want to advance in the organization, get this now: your development is your own baby. Always initiate discussions with your manager about your development.

Schedule a few minutes meeting with your organisation's Head of Learning & Development for advice, volunteer to do other projects to learn, whatever it takes, just do it. It's your personal individual responsibility so just take it upon yourself and never expect anyone else to be concerned with your development except you. It's all in your hands my friend. You determine how far you go and the time it takes to get there.

37. "TO ACHIEVE MORE THAN AN AVERAGE PERSON, YOU MUST WORK LONGER AND HARDER THAN THE AVERAGE PERSON." BRIAN TRACY

Many people don't actually realise how much you have to work to break into a different level in an organisation or in terms of your economic/social class. Many studies have proven that economic mobility is extremely difficult. The world system is designed to keep you in the same economic class you were born in. For example, if you were born into a working class family and all you do every day is wake up, go to work, come back, watch TV and sleep, you will most likely die in that class, unfortunately so.

You have to seriously change your thinking, actions and habits in order to break into a different economic class. You have to be much more forceful and intentional about it. You have to put in the necessary effort, long hours and sacrifices. Similarly, you ought to be more determined to breaking barriers impeding your progress. This means saying no to mediocrity and average performance. It means saying no to blending with the masses. It means choosing to add value and working harder and longer than the rest.

38. YOU MUST PEOPLE AT WORK; BEING SEEN WITH THEM WILL COST YOU THE PROMOTION YOU WANT

Organisations have all kinds of people and personalities and this is one of the factors that make the work environment so dynamic and diverse. Some of us are naturally sociable and we like people, but in the work environment, not everyone can and should be your friend. There are some people that you should be allergic to, so you should avoid them at all costs, simply because they will hinder your progress.

I read an article published on Inc.Com written by Lolly Daska, President and CEO of Lead From Within and she says people who display the following symptoms are the kind you should avoid at work:

1. TOXIC ARROGANCE
There is a big difference between confidence and

arrogance. Confidence inspires whereas arrogance intimidates. Arrogant people always know best and feel superior to others. They will never celebrate your confidence because it interferes with their arrogance.

2. TOXIC VICTIMHOOD

Some of the most dangerous people you can have around you are the perpetual victims. These are people who look at their own issues and mistakes and always find others to blame. They lack accountability and will thus blame everyone else for their shortfalls, from their unloving parents to their current partners and ultimately you, whether as a friend or colleague.

Toxic victims never take ownership of their mistakes and lives in general. It's always because someone else did 'this' which led him or her to doing 'that.' It's never just, I did that, I made a mistake, I was wrong and I will face the consequences and resolve this.

3. TOXIC CONTROL

Controlling people know everything and the best way to do anything. However, they are usually very insecure beneath it all. The problem with hanging around the toxic controllers is that as long as they are around you, you will never get a chance to voice out an idea or do anything yourself.

4. TOXIC ENVY

Those plagued with jealousy are never happy with what they have. Most of us keep them in our circles anyway yet become surprised when they are not as happy as we thought they would be for us, for our achievements and successes. Our logic is that they may be envious but they are our friends after all so we ought to expect them to rejoice with and for us. Can you really blame them though?

I mean if they are generally discontent and unhappy with whatever they have and wherever they are, how do you expect them to be happy when good things happen to you? They simply lack that ability, they can't appreciate it when others achieve or move forward. They often feel that if anything good is going to happen, it should happen to them. They are the 'cream of the crop' and only they deserve the best after all.

5. TOXIC LIARS

As long as there are people, there will be liars. Chronic liars are harmful though because you never know what to believe, so you can't count on their word; neither can you count on their promises. They will lie to you about others and thus lie to others about you; it is what it is.

6. TOXIC NEGATIVITY

You probably know someone who's always angry, resentful and suspicious of everything. Negativity destroys relationships and spending time with negative people will make you feel they are sucking the life out of you. For peace and progress sake, stay away!

7. TOXIC GREED

So much of our culture tells us to want more, achieve more and earn more. To a certain degree, that kind of desire and ambition can be good, but it becomes problematic when 'wanting' becomes toxic. This is because when toxic people want something, they want it all – that which is theirs and that which is not alike. Moreover, when they have anything in abundance, rather than doing or being kind to others, the focus is solely on them and their lives.

8. TOXIC JUDGMENT

There's a big difference between making a judgment and being judgmental. Judgments are objective and based on discernment whereas being judgmental is about criticism. Judgmental people are always quick to jump to conclusions. They are poor listeners and communicators.

9. TOXIC GOSSIP

Gossipers see themselves as having a deep conversation about someone, an exchange of information. They do it to elevate themselves above their insecurity and there's no distinction between speculation and fact. Few things are more destructive than gossip. Talking about the other will never change nor improve anything about yourself or circumstances. If anything, the more you gossip, the more critical and harsh you become, which hinders you from learning from others and allowing yourself to grow as a result.

10. TOXIC LACK OF CHARACTER

When someone lacks integrity and honesty, that is, when cheating, lying, manipulating, gossiping and greed are part of the norm, there are few things these people won't do to get their way. If they decide you're an obstacle to them, they'll come after you with everything they have. Be careful of people who have limited barriers and a silent conscience, they will destroy you.

39. STOP YOUR OBSESSION WITH HAVING FUN. FUN WILL LIMIT YOUR PROGRESS

For some of us, the reason we don't see progress in our lives is simple: we are just more committed to having fun than to our own development. I mean seriously, it's not compulsory to go clubbing every weekend, going out to chill and hanging out just for fun, attending concerts, watching movies and whatever else we do for fun. Sometimes you just need to sit yourself down and do that assignment or research you've been threatening to do. Obsession with fun will hinder your progress.

When South Africa's DJ Shimza and Dr Malinga produced the song with the line: *'akulalwa; si jaiva ubusuku bonke'* meaning we don't sleep, we party all night long, we must contrarily say *'akulalwa; sisebenza ubusuku bonke'* meaning we don't sleep; we work all night long. I'm not criticising these artists or their song –

their work ethic is actually quite exemplary. I'm merely using this to challenge those of us who spend 80% of our time partying and chilling and then wonder why we never progress.

If you have time for everything else except the tasks that you should do yet never do, then sooner or later, fun becomes a norm and fun is all that you're about; it literally encompasses everything about you. Please don't become that person! Refuse to be about that life, it's not worth it, not when you have so much potential and such big dreams.

You can't afford to compromise yourself, your ambitions and destiny like that. Refuse to be the person everyone knows to call when they are bored or want something to do because they know you are always game for anything. If you need to grow a backbone, grow it in this area. You can't be a yes man or woman in this regard, be disciplined. Know your priorities and set them, let them be known and stick to them without compromise. Fun is necessary yes, but fun can't be the most predominant element of our lives comrades, not if we want to get ahead and progress in this life. If progress is what we want then fun is an element worth compromising now and again. Remember as I said earlier, progress requires effort and determination. Progress also requires sacrifice so let's be realistic, what's a bit of fun compared to the results we will reap if we fully apply ourselves, commit to our personal development and utilise our utmost potential?

I believe it will be worthwhile so think long-term. Most of us loose out on significant valuable time because when it comes to fun, our thinking is like a short circuit.

Here are three significant truths about fun to remember before choosing fun over work:

1. There is something called too much fun.
2. Fun never runs out, it will always be there.
3. You can never exhaust fun; it only exhausts you.

This is because fun often comes at a price and compromise of our sleep, rest and ultimately, exhaustion, which hampers our performance and functioning even days after the few hours of fun that we had.

Therefore, consider this a warning: if you continue with this fun over work mentality and lifestyle, if you continue playing more than you work, if your 80/20 rule means 80% fun and 20% work then trust me, poverty will attack you like an armed robber!

Please don't get me twisted here, I'm not saying we must lead boring and *fun-less* lives because we are only concerned with our progress. On the contrary, we do need that thrill and excitement or else we will quickly exhaust our mileage and get burnt out so I'm not suggesting that you do that to yourself. I'm merely saying we must watch how much of our time, resources, our lives and ultimately ourselves we give to fun.

Some of you are supposed to be managers, directors and CEOs by now. You are supposed to have your company up and running, featured on Forbes magazine and a guest on popular radio and TV shows, but your obsession with fun keeps obstructing and buffering your progress.

Let us re-evaluate our standpoint regarding what fun means and how much fun we can afford to have. If you are honest enough with and to yourself and admittedly realise that you have been off track and side-tracked by fun, then it's time to reroute my friend. Change your current location and navigate back to where you ought to be and find your way back to progress.

40. PEOPLE JUDGE YOU HARSHLY WHEN YOU ARE UNTESTED, IT'S NOT PERSONAL. FOCUS ON THE WORK AND MOST WILL COME AROUND

When I wrote Bulls & Bears: life lessons from the financial markets, I mentioned this point. When former President Thabo Mbeki was inaugurated as president in 1999, the rand fell to more than R6.00 to the dollar for the first time (it's hard to believe but the rand was averaging about R3.50 to the dollar in 1994). The rand fell even further when Tito Mboweni was appointed Governor of the South African Reserve Bank. Is it not interesting that the same people who were nervous when Thabo Mbeki was elected president and Tito

Mboweni was appointed governor are now praising both men for fiscal discipline?

People now miss both men, the same men they initially ridiculed. Those who were nervous are now their biggest fans. This is the same thing that will happen with you when you get a new role. People will get nervous, they will criticise you and some won't even give you the support you need and deserve. This has very little to do with you as a person so it's normal. Keep quiet, work hard, prove yourself and you will see those who were your critics turn into major fans.

41. LET THE ANALYSTS TALK; FOCUS ON THE WORK AT HAND. FOCUSING ON THE NOISE WILL LIMIT YOUR PROGRESS

When Maria Ramos took over as CEO of Barclays Africa (then ABSA) from Steven Booysens in 2009, most analysts thought it was a bad decision. She has since grown the bank's Return on Equity from 13.23 in 2009 to 16.50. Ironically, the same analysts now believe she will be the right candidate to replace Antony Jenkins as CEO of Barclays plc.

Lesson in all this: it's always easier to analyse than to do. Let the analysts talk while you relentlessly execute your vision to progress in life.

42. DON'T LET ANYONE MAKE YOU FEEL YOU ARE LESS AMBITIOUS IF YOU WANT TO CLIMB THE CORPORATE LADDER INSTEAD OF STARTING YOUR OWN BUSINESS

It's a well-known fact that South Africa has a very low entrepreneurial culture and I understand that we need to change that. However, it appears that the predominant method used to encourage this change has been to imply that people who want to work in Corporate SA are boring and that they lack ambition and determination in life.

We must not create an impression that having a corporate job is boring, that people who work in corporate lack ambition and initiative. We need strong people in Corporate SA as well. If you know that this running your own business thing is not for you, please don't feel pressured to start one. Enjoy your corporate career to the fullest. The money is good as well; I used to work in HR so I know.

43. MONEY DOES MATTER

Don't make the mistake of listening to the 'money doesn't matter; just follow your passion' crowd. I've studied a lot of models on choosing a career and I still think Jim Collin's model is one of the best as it's much more comprehensive, realistic and practical.

He calls it The Hedgehog Concept and a significant question to ask yourself is this: are you engaged in work that fits your own three circles?

1.   What are you passionate about?
2.   What are you genetically encoded for?
3.   What can you get paid for?

Here's the good news, you don't have to choose between these three, and all you need is to get your sweet spot.

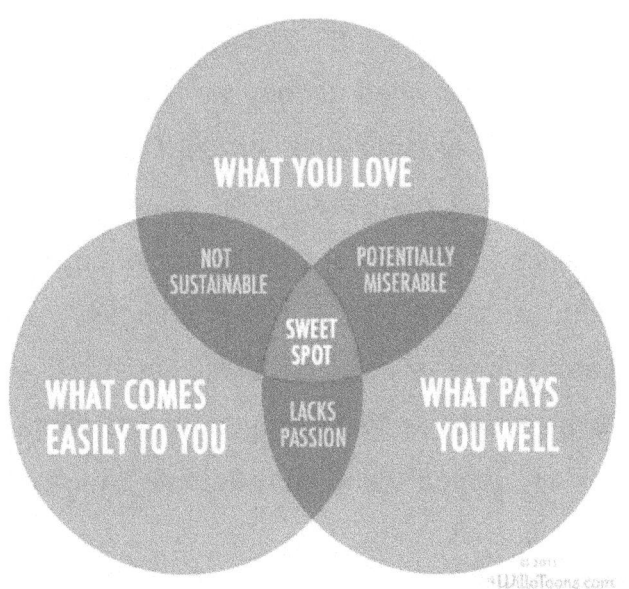

Source: *Willowtoons.com as adapted from Jim Collin's 'Good to Great.'*

44. IF YOU ARE IN THE 'GIG ECONOMY,' UNDERSTAND THAT ALL SEASONS EVENTUALLY END

The gig economy is basically the freelancing economy. These are people who work for different employers without any exclusivity rights. There was a time when this was a terrain for artists and professional speakers like me but the dynamic nature of employment has led to more and more people opting to be freelancers.

If you are in the 'gig economy' then you will know that there are seasons when nobody wants to invite you to sing, speak or whatever else you do. Don't doubt your gift because of a dry season. All seasons eventually end. Likewise, there will be times when you are flourishing and the star of the company or your manager but there will also be a time when you are just doing okay or not so well even. Embrace all seasons like, they all eventually end and alternate after all.

45. EXPAND YOUR THINKING; DEAL WITH THE LIMITATIONS IN YOUR MIND

On Friday the 11th of September 2015, I achieved something very significant. You see up until then, I had never set foot in a Lamborghini dealership. I've always been very afraid to do it. I often questioned if I'm worthy to go there. So that Friday on my way to a meeting, I decided to sign in (yes you sign in) at the Lamborghini and Bentley dealership on William Nicol drive in Bryanston, Johannesburg and confidently walked onto the floor and viewed those machines in close proximity.

I made a serious shift in mindset that day. This is how it all starts after all. I still don't own it but finally, I can actually comprehend owning one. This is the shift that we all need to make in order to progress in life. Deal with the limitations in your own mind. Can you comprehend being in the top ten percent of the people in your field? Can you comprehend being the most senior accountant in your company? Can you comprehend being a partner at one of the big five auditing firms in the world?

Recently, I watched a TED Talk of someone I grew up with, Dr Patience Mthunzi who is a senior researcher at the Human Science Research Council. She's currently spearheading global research on the ability to cure HIV with lasers. From the dusty streets of Soweto, she is recognized globally for her work. It is possible.

A South African company such as Aspen Holdings also inspires me in this manner. It started in South Africa and became so global that currently, less than 25% of its earnings come from SA. Aspen is now a supplier of branded and generic pharmaceuticals and nutritional products in more than 150 countries across the world. They have selected their territories and are dominating them.

My thinking has become global as well. No more tiny little dreams of opening a *spaza* shop. We think global now. Can you comprehend it? Change your thinking.

> *"If you put yourself in a position where you have to stretch outside your comfort zone, then you are forced to expand your consciousness."*
> **Les Brown**
>
> *"The world we see that seems so insane is the result of a belief system that is not working. To perceive the world differently, we must be willing to change our belief system, let the past slip away, expand our sense of now, and dissolve the fear in our minds."*
> **William James**

46. AFTER YOU CHANGE YOUR THINKING, HAVE A WORK ETHIC TO MATCH IT

In the previous point, I asked if you could comprehend being in the top ten percent of people in your field. An interesting and noteworthy point about people who are in the top ten percent of their field though is that when you've both put in a lot of work, you go celebrate and they continue to work.

I was actually thinking about this recently during a conference of professional speakers around the world in Washington DC, United States. People who are on top of their game surrounded me in that conference. I came back home and was slightly frustrated. All of us want to hang around successful people but often hanging around with people on top of their game can be very frustrating. You start to realize that the reason you don't operate at that level is actually not racism, favouritism, nepotism or any other 'isms.' The reason is YOU. That is obviously frustrating because it is much easier to blame the 'isms' and much harder to admit that YOU are the problem. You have a weak work ethic;

you are not disciplined enough. You have too many excuses and and and! You see if you're going to progress, you have to modify and fine-tune your work ethic.

I laughed so hard recently when I was emceeing the National Talent Management Conference and one of the speakers was Dr Marko Saravanja, the Chairman of Regenesys Business School who said, "You don't have to be intelligent to get a PhD, believe me I have one." He made a point that all you really need is a healthy work ethic and discipline.

I prepare most of my speeches and do most of my writing at 3 O'clock in the morning, for example. When most people wake up, I'm already about three hours ahead. Create a work ethic that will not only match but also sustain and continuously improve your role and position.

47. PREPARE FOR LINEAR CAREER PROGRESSION BUT LEAVE SOME ROOM FOR DIVINE INTERVENTION

Often as human beings, we tend to think career progression will be linear (progressing from one stage to another in a single series of steps). In other words, I will be an Agent, then a Team Leader, and then a Manager; whichever order your industry applies.

Believe it or not, God can elevate you in a non- linear way. He can cause you to skip some steps and still give you the grace to handle that new level. Prepare for linear progression but leave space for divine intervention. I know we all have different beliefs but never overlook nor undermine the spiritual element to career progression.

48. RELENTLESS PREPARATION WILL CAUSE YOU TO BE SEEN NEXT TO THE BEST IN THE WORLD

Until the 27th August 2015, many South Africans (including me) didn't know who Anaso Jobondwana was. And then in what seemed to be all of a sudden, out of nowhere, we woke up to that iconic picture of Anaso Jobondwana running next to Usain Bolt during the 15th IAAF World Championships at the National Stadium in Beijing, China.

I say it seemed all of a sudden because to us, it seemed that way but for Anaso, who had been preparing for that moment in obscurity, it wasn't sudden at all. Relentless preparation will allow you to be seen next to the best in the world. As you continue to work hard in obscurity, keep your determination and persistence. Nobody might know you and no-one may want to give you a chance BUT one day, you will appear next to the best in the world and everyone will be like: "Where did he come from?" Just like Johnny Walker, keep going because your time will surely come.

What you do in obscurity will eventually bring you to the spotlight.

49. YOUR OPPORTUNITY WILL SURELY COME

At times it may seem like everyone else is being promoted and advancing in his or her career except you. In such times, you need to be reminded that your opportunity will surely come. It may be delayed but eventually it will come into being. Keep doing the right things and mixing the right ingredients: plan, prepare, work hard and it will surely come.

There was a certain organisation that always asked me to quote them to facilitate certain workshops for them but never really gave me the opportunity. A friend of mine asked me why I still quote them because they are using me to comply with the 'three quotes requirement' and I told him that I'm aware that they just want to have three quotes. I'm also aware that they have their favourite facilitator.

I know though that one day their favourite facilitator will be unavailable to conduct the workshop and they will have to use me. It's like a goalkeeper patiently waiting for his chance, I said to him. About two months ago, it actually happened, they asked me to speak at one of their conferences. I was so emotional when it happened, remembering what I told my friend.

I presented that speech as if I was about to die. In my subconscious, I wanted them to forget their favourite – I'm still waiting for that second call.   Your opportunity will come. I've asked this question and I will ask it again: will you be ready when it comes? Remember preparation comes before the presented opportunity. When opportunity comes, it's too late to prepare, start now as though it has already been presented.

50. DO YOU WANT TO KNOW WHO'S RESPONSIBLE FOR THE LACK OF PROGRESS IN YOUR LIFE? LOOK IN THE MIRROR

"An important decision I made was to resist playing the Blame Game. The day I realized that I am in charge of how I will approach problems in my life, that things will turn out better or worse because of me and nobody else, that was the day I knew I would be a happier and healthier person. And that was the day I knew I could truly build a life that matters." Steve Goodier

"The problem is NOT funding, the problem is me." I came to this conclusion in 2004 when I was running my first business, Amakhono Esizwe. I submitted my business plan to a few development finance institutions and they all declined my application. I cried racism. I cried corruption. I blamed everything and everyone else until one day, I saw a business plan of someone who was actually funded and at that point I realised that the problem was not 'out there' but within me.

I saw what a quality business plan looked like and to be honest, mine was sloppy, to say the least. Sometimes we have to look in the mirror before we blame everyone and everything else. The answer is often closer to us than we think so look in the mirror first before you look out there.

"Blaming others is an act of refusing to take responsibility. When a person can't accept the fact or the reality, they blamed another person or the situation instead of taking accountability."
Dee Dee Atner

"Blame doesn't empower you. It keeps you stuck in a place you don't want to be because you don't want to make the temporary, but painful decision, to be responsible for the outcome of your own life's happiness."
Shannon L. Alder

---

51. STUDY THE LANGUAGE THAT HAS WEIGHT AND SPEAK IT

In every organisation, there's a language that has weight. I spent a big portion of my working life working in banks and I realised very early that if you want to catch the attention of executives in the bank, you have to understand "bank speak". I was fortunate enough to be chosen to study an international certificate in retail banking and after that, how senior people viewed me changed because I could speak their language. Find out what the language that has weight is in your organisation and learn it fast. It will propel your progress.

52. LEARN TO MIND YOUR OWN BUSINESS

If I ever had to choose a mantra I live by, it would have to be this: make it your ambition to lead a quiet life, to mind your own business, and to work with your own hands. Many people care too much about other people's business and neglect their own.

When you are at work, please remember that you are there for yourself and not anyone else. Stay out of office dramas and if possible, avoid office politics and office romance, most never end well. Most importantly though, don't be the cause of all that drama and politics by sniffing your nose where it doesn't belong.

In minding your own business, teach others to mind their own too. Remember at the end of the day, work is work and it's significant to maintain professionalism in how you generally carry yourself and most importantly, in manner of speech, attitude and actions. Make it your mission to watch what, how and who you say it to. Unfortunately some people will stop at nothing to get ahead, even if it means disclosing personal information to bad-mouth, sabotage and ruin your reputation.

It's also very important to remember that such disclosure may easily be done deliberately or unconsciously as some people may share your personal information for the right reasons but unfortunately to the wrong person. It's therefore important to keep your business to yourself, especially that which puts you in a professionally vulnerable position. These are cases in which your performance and chances for a promotion may be affected and sabotaged.

The tip is to never give anyone ammunition against yourself, so be very careful whom you open up to and the details you disclose.

53. WE ALL NEED INSPIRATION – FIND SOMETHING OR SOMEONE THAT INSPIRES YOU

I don't want to get into religion because this book is for everyone but I have to tell you a story that was a great inspiration to me.

I think the day was Sunday the 13th of February 2005. Our church landlord at the community hall in Orange Farm Extension 2 had told us that we couldn't use the hall on that day. So we were using a smaller, dodgy hall and combined it with a tent to have a Sunday service. It was raining, the roof was leaking and the mood was a bit sombre, as you can imagine.

Our Pastor, who happens to be my dad, my role model, my mentor and inspiration, then arrived. As he was about to preach someone (I can't remember who), made an announcement that our Pastor had just received his PhD. and it will be conferred to him soon. Before that moment, I had never known anyone with a PhD. Suddenly, the mood changed. Suddenly, many of us believed it was possible. That moment changed my life. That moment was my divine 'aha' moment.

We all need inspiration and most of the time, its right in our nose and thus we need not to look any further. Someone need not be older or famous to inspire you, I have received inspiration from those my age and younger alike, if you open your heart to it, you will receive that inspiration, whichever form it comes in.

54. IGNORING THE INVISIBLE FENCES

A pet fence or fenceless boundary is an electronic system designed to keep a pet or other domestic animals within a set of predefined boundaries without the use of a 'real or physical fence'. A mild electronic shock is delivered as and when the pet tries to cross the boundary. The pet soon learns to avoid the invisible fence location, making it an effective virtual barrier. In Psychological Learning Theories the fence is a stimulus that elicits a response, which in time becomes so reinforced, it is unconsciously elicited even.

Unfortunately as human beings, we also suffer from the Invisible Fence Syndrome (IFS), I just invented a psychological disorder. Who knows, maybe someday it will make it to the Diagnostic and Statistical Manual of Mental Disorders. Well let's move on to elaborate on how the IFS works; the key symptom is in giving up and quitting based on past experience. The invisible fence exists because every time you try to do something and fail, you start believing there's a boundary and that you must not even attempt to break it in order to avoid negative feedback. Ultimately, you learn that you shouldn't even attempt to cross because chances are, you won't make it to the other side.

Some of you have applied so many times for that position that you don't even want to apply anymore. You don't want to try anymore. Let me share the good news, the key fact about learning is that we can both learn and unlearn. Therefore, because we learn to avoid the cross over, we can unlearn the crossover avoidance and *relearn* to attempt and keep attempting until we make it. Today, I would like to say to you; there is NO fence, there is NO boundary and there is NO limit. Cross OVER my friend. Try again. Go for it.

55. UNDERSTAND THAT OTHERS WILL TRY TO HINDER YOUR PROGRESS – TOUGHEN UP

Some people enter the workplace with a very naïve mentality, thinking everyone cares about them, their issues and successes. As a result, they tend to open up and trust a bit too much, unknowingly to the wrong person or crowd. Unfortunately this naïve mindset is delusional and may hamper your career progress and success.

The fact is this, in a work environment, relationships play out a bit differently. Work is not home and your colleagues are not really your family or friends. Therefore, not everyone cares about you, your career and getting you ahead. Unfortunately not everyone has your best interests at heart and not everyone will look out for you nor want you to get ahead. Therefore, you can't rely on everyone to progress and get ahead in your career, sometimes not even your colleague buddies or manager for that matter.

In fact, people, friends and enemies, or rather 'frenemies' will try to sabotage and block your progress. They will bad-mouth you, jeopardise your work and even misrepresent you. It may look like they are succeeding for a while but NO ONE can block your progress permanently. NO ONE! The best you can do is toughen up and snap out of your 'naïve-hood.' Understand and accept that you just have to trust and rely on yourself more. Please understand that I'm not suggesting that you possess a 'me against the world' kind of attitude because some people genuinely care and want what's best for you. I'm just saying you must be tough enough to realise that some people can be a wolf under a sheepskin and it's your responsibility to protect yourself and stay away.

When they eventually become revealed to you, do not hate, resent nor be bitter. Merely understand that it's just part of the life package and work dynamics so be courageous and tough enough to walk away in peace and avoid vengeance.

56. HAVE BIAS FOR ACTION

"I thought about if first" is the language of regret. Don't regret sitting on your idea without putting action to it. Be known as person who does things and not one who talks about things.

"Well done is much better than well said."
Benjamin Franklin

"One of these days is none of these days".
English proverb

Don't be that type of person who say, "I will do it one of these days"; just do it.

57. BE THE CREAM OF THE CROP IN YOUR FIELD – BE THE BEST

There is really not much I can say to make this point. To set yourself up for career progression and advancement simply means you ought to do your best all the time. The difference between the cream of the crop and the masses simply lies in the fact that what the cream of the crop do every day is what the masses do once in a while.

So don't be a once-off hard worker but work hard all the time. This doesn't mean you must be at work from 8am to 8pm all day, every day; you still have a life right.

The point is to establish yourself as one who excels in all they do, no matter how small or minute the tasks may seem. Be known as the go-to person where excellence and the best results are required.

58. WHEN YOU GET THAT BIG PROMOTION THAT SCARES YOU, DON'T CHICKEN OUT

Promotions are frightening, particularly if you've been an exceptional performer on your current level. You are used to being the star and all of a sudden, you are not fully performing because you are new. It may be tempting to tell your boss that you want your old job back, in fact it's normal to feel like that but don't chicken out – it will be much better in a few months' time.

There's a psychological concept called habituation, which is the same phenomenon used in the swimming analogy. When you get into the swimming pool for the first time on any day, the water may feel very cold but several minutes later, you have adapted and it feels okay and normal even. Likewise, it may be a bit scary, overwhelming and challenging at first but once you get the hang of things, you will habituate and get used to it. Don't be so hard on yourself; all in good time my friend.

59. SCHEDULE TIME IN YOUR DIARY TO THINK ABOUT YOUR CAREER DEVELOPMENT

Whatever is scheduled will be done. If you simply keep thinking of how you need to think about your career development yet never make time to actually think about it and plan, then you are as good as the employee who wastes time on social media, idle chatting with colleagues and other unnecessary things when they have a deadline coming up. They will keep finding excuses and justifying their actions and never really get to the work until it's too late and the pressure is too high.

Never allow pressure to force you to thinking and planning for your career development. It's better to start thinking of it now before it becomes a must because when it becomes a necessity, then you know you are not in a good place. Think and plan in advance, make the time because nobody will make it for you nor think about your own development on your behalf.

60. DON'T COMPROMISE YOUR CONTINUOUS PROFESSIONAL DEVELOPMENT (CPD)

Continuous professional development simply means consistent and non-stop learning and self-enhancement in your career and industry. It means you are devoted to improving your knowledge and skills; that you are open to innovation and implementing new strategies, systems and processes to keep up with the times. Who would want to be operated by a surgeon who last developed him/herself in 1981? Nobody!

Refuse to be irrelevant and out-dated. Save yourself from the headache of forcing to do things as they have always been done whilst working with people who want to do things the 2015 way with a 2020 mentality. Keep current. Stay on top of your game. Read on your industry research and current trends and commit yourself to implementation. Never settle nor think you have reached your peak because wherever you are, there is always an opportunity to learn, grow and fully apply yourself. You never reach your destination until you die.

61. IMPROVE YOUR EDUCATION/SKILL

Consider the following graphic:

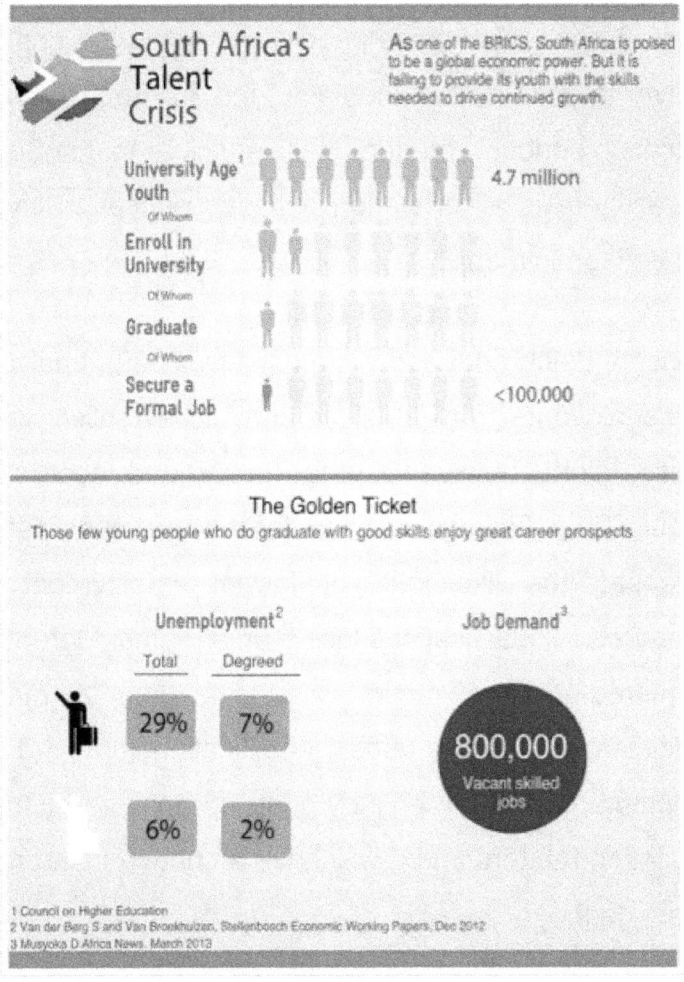

Source: mindoverminerals.com

I know there's a school of thought that has emerged claiming that education is not important because we can succeed without it. Proponents of this argument often tell us about people such as Steve Jobs and Bill Gates. I don't think these people are wrong but context really matters in this instance and in South Africa, education seriously matters. It is very clear that in South Africa, there is a correlation between education levels and economic mobility.

Branson, Leibbrandt and Zuzu (Cloete; 2009), analysed household data from 2000 to 2007 to establish clear, positive links between further study and access to labour. Their findings showed that matric qualification increased the likelihood of formal employment as compared to qualifications less than a matric. Moreover, compared to the group with less than a matric certificate, obtaining a tertiary qualification improved the likelihood of formal employment up to three times. Education matters and if you have a chance to improve yours, do it.

Another important element to add here is dedicated to the adults. You may be in a great comfortable job and role with a great salary, and whether you went to school or not is besides the point, the point is that wherever you are, whatever your academic history and however you got that job, it's never too late to learn and enhance yourself.

You may be doing your job well and know all you think there is to know about it but trust me, you can never know enough so don't close yourself up to learning. It doesn't even have to be an intense full-on qualification; taking short classes to enhance yourself, develop your skill set and just being informed about your industry and work role can never do you any harm, try it and see for yourself. It will actually do you wonders and intensify your interest.

62. DEVELOP A CAREER PLAN

This sounds very fluffy but it is absolutely critical.

Allow me to share with you my career plan, which I developed in 2011 as a guideline. As most things, it has changed but it is still a good guideline:

Career Plan 2011-2021 (10-year plan)

Year	Age	Position	Skills to Learn	Anticipated Salary
2021	40 +	CEO of my own people development company and full-time speaker.	Professional Speaking	R4m+
2018-2021 (3 years)	38-40	Group HR Director in financial services or engineering company	Executive Education	R2m
2016-2018 (3 years)	35-38	Chief Learning Officer in financial services or engineering company	Executive Education Relationships	R1.4m
2013-2015 (3 years)	32-34	EXCO level role (Head of Cluster/Segment L&D in a bank or Head of Divisional HR)	HR Practices Study Talent Management & Labour Law	R1m
2011-2012 2years)	30-31	Snr. Manager: Learning & Development	Current Position	

I'm not sure that those anticipated salaries are 100% accurate but it was very important for me to also plan what I wanted to earn. I think it's very important for all of us. What has since happened with me is that I left Corporate South Africa earlier than I planned in order to pursue my vision of being a CEO of my business and full-time professional speaker.

I'm nowhere close to earning my target salary but it's important to have a vision and see it through. There may be tweaks here and there but having a guideline is always better than no guideline at all. A guideline will serve as a constant reminder for your desired outcome and keep you on track instead of allowing yourself to be swayed and blown by every passing wind.

If you are young and reading this book, consider yourself blessed because you have an impactful tool. One of the reasons I'm actually writing this book is for you, young person because I wish I had a manual like this when I was younger. I am thus honoured to present this to you and inspire you to structure your career and progression goals.

The thing about being young is that most of you prefer going with the flow and just taking things as they come, which is okay but unfortunately that can be a disadvantage to your career. Most of you tend to just enter the workplace without a clear vision and career plan, which is understandable as universities don't teach this but now that you have the knowledge, use it.

Find out what you want and where you want to be then plan to get there and see it through so that you don't unnecessarily find yourself in 10 different jobs within 10 different companies in a very few years. As I mentioned earlier, width is great but depth is an absolute necessity to your career progression, especially if you aim to be in the corporate sector for long and want to be in a senior managerial position that pays you a high-end salary.

63. DON'T LET YOUR CAREER GOALS BE A SECRET – TALK TO YOUR BOSS ABOUT THEM

When I knew that I wanted to be a professional speaker, I spoke to my then boss about it. That was one of the best decisions I have ever made. Knowing that I am a good performer, she allowed me to speak at a very small meeting with some of our team leaders. The title of my talk was 'Help; I'm a team leader.'

After that talk, she received feedback that I added so much value so she asked me to draft a proposal, which was to be sent to EXCO for me to present motivational talks for all staff members in our division. That ladies and gentlemen, launched my professional speaking career. Every time I tell her that she played a major role in my speaking career, she brushes me off, but I know as well as I know my name that she did and I'm eternally grateful.

I know some bosses will not support you like she supported me. Maybe they won't go to that extent but please talk to your boss about your career ambitions in the company, chances are that he/she has the ability to make it happen.

64. BECOME AN INTRAPRENEUR — VIEW YOUR JOB AS A CONSULTING ASSIGNMENT, NOT A PERMANENT GIG

An intrapreneur is defined as "a person who while remaining within a larger organization uses entrepreneurial skills to develop a new product or line of business as a subsidiary of the organization" (dictionaryreference.com).

This is how carrercast.com puts it; "Years ago, Fast Company Magazine had a cover story called 'Me, Inc.' which revolutionised its readers' thinking about their careers. The article said that because organisations no longer guarantee lifetime employment, it's important to think of yourself as a contractor with a portfolio instead of a loyal employee.

As a contractor, your focus should be doing excellent work, learning as much as possible from each position, and being ready to hop to a new job should the desire or need arise." If you treat your job like this, you are more likely going to add more value and therefore advance your career.

65. DON'T BE TOO CAUTIOUS – TAKE SOME RISK

Be innovative. Take risks. Always be on the lookout for problems in the organisation and do your best to find solutions even if they are not in your direct control. I can assure you that senior leadership will always want to meet the staff member who solved a problem.

66. ASK FOR MORE WORK OR MORE RESPONSIBILITIES

"Volunteering to help out other departments or teams — or simply asking for more responsibilities increases your value within the organization. Asking for additional work shows an interest and desire to help your department and company to succeed. It also puts a spotlight on your value to the business." (Allbusiness)

67. JOIN A PROFESSIONAL ASSOCIATION RELEVANT TO YOU AND WHEN YOU GET THERE, VOLUNTEER TO DO SOMETHING

Associations look great on your CV and are helpful networks to tap into when searching for a job. Don't wait until you need the support, get involved right away and start building those relationships. My involvement at the South African Board for People Practices and at the Professional Speakers Association of Southern Africa has really contributed to my career growth. When I tell some people, they always say their employer refuses to pay for their membership fee. If I were you, I would just pay for myself – it is worth it.

68. FIND A MENTOR INSIDE THE ORGANISATION AND ANOTHER ONE OUTSIDE

When it comes to selecting a mentor, the greatest likelihood is that the person you are considering gets many requests for mentorship, which is why you have to make sure yours stand out. Here are some few suggestions:

- Be an excellent performer in your current role. Every senior person wants to mentor a performer. If you can't even do your job, maybe you should focus on that.

- Be persistent but not irritating – there's a very thin line here. Follow the correct channels, be polite but don't give up when they decline you the first time. Remember that the person does not owe you anything.

- Show them something you are currently busy with and ask for input or proofreading. This is much better than the 'coffee request' invitation. It shows that you are not just a talker but also a doer.

- Make your proposal clear and be upfront about what is involved or required.

- When you eventually meet, shut up and listen. Many people use this opportunity to try and sell themselves and they waste the mentor's time. Humble yourself and learn.

69. YOU MUST PERFORM BUT YOU MUST ALSO BE SEEN TO BE PERFORMING

What is the use of doing something great for your organisation if no one will know about it? You must learn the art of self-promotion. I say art because that's exactly what it is. You have to do it in a subtle manner but accomplish the goal still. The trick is to be subtle yet effective, microscopic yet proactive.

You also have to select your crowd strategically by making sure the people who matter know what you have done. In Corporate South Africa, there are talent meetings/forums that are held regularly, make it your mission to ensure your name always appears there.

This is how not to do it: don't try to go over your boss by sending his/her boss emails; that is a plain career suicide bomb that will explode on your face so please find other creative ways to promote yourself. Many companies have sites where you can log innovative ideas, for example, attending every session where the

CEO is updating staff on results etc. and asking relevant questions. Do that instead.

The point is to be visible everywhere yet making sure you are still performing. You don't want to be in the spotlight when your work and performance rating doesn't deserve to be. Your work must shine just as bright so if you are to be seen and known, sloppy work and average performance can't be associated with you. To stand out as your own personal brand requires that you simultaneously produce work that is worthy of the spotlight. Align the two by ensuring your performance represents you well.

70. INVEST IN YOUR OWN DEVELOPMENT

When I was 25, I registered for an MBA and because I was too junior in my company to qualify for a bursary to study for an MBA, I paid for it myself, well, at least for the first two years. When I told some people, they said it was too expensive and asked how I was able to afford it. These were the same people who wore some really expensive shoes and paid about R2, 000 a month on clothing accounts from a net salary of around R4, 800.

I was paying about R2, 000 as well for my education and that MBA has definitely added a zero or two into my annual earnings. Invest in your development my friend – it always pays off so rather sacrifice the brands and top notch/'top shayela' lifestyle and resources.

71. SPEAK FOR FREE AT INDUSTRY CONFERENCES IF YOU HAVE SOMETHING TO SAY

I'm always amazed at a number of relatively senior people who don't do this. I mean seriously, nothing says 'he's an expert' like speaking in industry conferences. Of course you have to be relatively senior to do that but if you are allowed to do this in your organisation, start now. It will exceptionally raise your profile and position you as a value-adding employee.

72. WRITE ARTICLES AND SEND THEM TO THE MEDIA ALL THE TIME

Ask permission from your employers to write a regular article in 'your personal capacity' for newspapers and other professional and reputable sources of information. You can use this platform to discuss industry trends and give tips about relevant factors within your industry. What is interesting about this is that it allows you to shoot two birds with one stone by building your profile both in your company and in your industry at large.

Offer value and suddenly you are the 'go-to' person on that topic. Your internal bosses will struggle to ignore you if everyone outside is looking for you. The media will often want to know what you have published before they consider you so the best way to start is by blogging. You can start your own blog for free and post interesting content. That will surely put you in a good place for consideration.

73. UPDATE YOUR LINKEDIN PROFILE

I'm actually amazed at the number of people who don't have LinkedIn profiles at all. Those of us who are reasonably active on LinkedIn can't even comprehend this. How do you say you want to advance your career yet you don't even exist on this amazing platform? And then there is the second category of people that only registered there and all you see is a name and company they worked for 10 years ago. Really? My friend, this is really easy to implement – do it immediately. An updated LinkedIn profile is compulsory in this day and age. In many recruiters' eyes, if you don't exist online, you simply don't exist!

74. START DRESSING AND BEHAVING LIKE A PERSON IN THE NEXT LEVEL

If your next level is an Executive Committee (EXCO) role, you must then start observing how EXCO members in your organisation dress and behave. If they never take lunch breaks and only eat at their desks, do the same. If they wear a tie every day, start wearing one, if they carry a copy of the Business Day newspaper to work every day, subscribe and do the same. Even if you don't understand anything on that newspaper, read it, it will all start making sense eventually. Most significantly though, you would be communicating a very clear message – I want that job and I'm ready for it.

75. WORK YOURSELF OUT OF A POSITION TO GET A PROMOTION

Career progression can be a bit confusing; sometimes being the reliable specialist in your organisation can hamper your advancement. One way to outgrow your current position is by ridiculously excelling in it, i.e. doing it so well and without struggle. This proves a level of mastery and shows you are now ready for greater challenges and responsibilities. However, a twist to the coin is that if you are the only one in your division who's a specialist in a particular system, why would management risk promoting you and loose that skill? Every time they think of promoting you, they think about loosing that skill.

In this case, you must actually train other people. As the saying goes, 'if you're the only one who can do it, then you are not a good leader.' The point of leadership is empowering and enabling others to do it just as well so lead by training others and then once there's someone else with the same ability or potential, show your seniors that there's more to you than what they know. In this way, you show them that you can do far more than your current position and your promotion will not be considered a loss to your department.

76. EXIT AND RETURN SENIOR STRATEGY

Sometimes in an organisation where you started as an Administrator for example, people will always see you as Administrator no matter what you do. In this case, no matter how much you actually love that organisation, you must leave and get a senior role elsewhere. If you really love that organisation, you can always return years later as someone senior and you will be taken more seriously.

77. THE DOWNGRADE TO UPGRADE STRATEGY

Let me create a scenario. Say, you've completed a degree in Mechanical Engineering about five years ago but because you were struggling to get a job or an internship in mechanical engineering, you ended up taking a job as a Call Centre Agent at a bank. After three years of being an Agent, you were promoted to being a Team Leader and you now earn R10, 000.00 per month.

Suddenly you are offered a mechanical engineering internship at a very big company for R6, 500.00 per month. You have bills but you love Mechanical Engineering and you know in the long run, you would earn more if you take the internship. What do you do? I suggest you use what I call the 'downgrade to upgrade strategy.' Take the internship, downgrade your lifestyle (sell your car, move into a backroom somewhere) and just start all over again. I know it's not as easy as it sounds but trust me, you will be glad you did down the line.

78. GO HORIZONTAL TO GO VERTICAL

In some small organisations with a flat structure, getting a promotion can be very hard. This does not mean you cannot progress, it just means you must be willing to take certain jobs that are on the same level if they will enhance your experience. Sometimes you just have to go horizontal in order to go vertical, more like a downgrade for an upgrade, it always pays off in the end.

79. INVEST IN A PRESENTATION/COMMUNICATION SKILLS PROGRAM

Why anybody can still call communication/presentation skills a 'soft skill' is a phenomenon I will never understand. Often the reason many people don't advance in their career is because they are really poor communicators. You might know your job in and out but if you can't communicate, your advancement is limited.

Don't let this so called 'soft skill' hinder your progress, read and write about anything that interests you, take a communications class, both theoretical and practical if possible. Read on and attend effective communications forums that will give you an opportunity to present and receive feedback so you can develop and improve yourself.

80. KNOW THE DEGREES, UNIVERSITIES AND LEARNING PROGRAMS THAT ARE VALUED IN YOUR COMPANY

I've worked as a Head of Learning/Training & Development in a few organisations and I can tell you this without any fear of contradiction whatsoever, every organisation has degrees, universities and learning programs that are held in high esteem. If you attend a certain program or do a particular degree in that institution, you improve your chances of advancement in that organisation.

It is your job to know what these are for your organisation and it is not that hard to find that information. Senior Managers, Human Resources and Heads of Learning and Development know them – the time to have that discussion with them is here and now.

81. SPEAK UP

If you are going to attend meetings and keep quiet for the entire session then the message is clear: you lack knowledge and there's nothing you can say that everyone else doesn't know. In order to be an active participant, you must firstly be knowledgeable about that subject matter and you have to speak up. Nobody really knows what you know so it's important to share your knowledge.

Most organisations have project teams that meet regularly until that particular project is implemented. In these project meetings, you find representatives from all departments who are needed for the launch of that project. What an opportunity this is for people to know you and to know what you know. Don't only speak when you have to give feedback about your department, give other suggestions that could add value. A huge disclaimer though: you have to know what you are talking about otherwise you will achieve the opposite of what you intended to achieve.

82. KNOW MORE ABOUT THE COMPANY, NOT JUST YOUR DIVISION

When I worked for a big bank, I was always surprised by how little people knew about the company they work for. Some people didn't even know which cluster their business belonged to, yet claimed they wanted to progress in that company. What a shock! When you don't know a lot about your company, you tend to think that the only way for you to progress is for your manager to leave, die or something of that sort.

Let me take this moment to inform you that you don't have to wait for such a time because there are always more opportunities than you think in your organisation. To have information access though, you have to know the company you work for in and out. You have to study your annual reports, your financial statements, newsletters etc. How else are you supposed to add value?

83. UNDERSTAND YOUR ORGANISATION'S POLITICS

I was attending a seminar one day and the speaker said, "Make it your mission to understand who plays golf with who, who goes to church with who and who went to high school with who in your organisation." When I heard that I thought to myself, surely this is an exaggeration; we are just there to work and nothing else. I have since learned that it is important not to be ignorant of workplace dynamics. I wouldn't go to the length that other people go to but it is important.

You see understanding these relationships and dynamics will help you in your progression movement as it will inform you on how to relate with who and power dynamics that indicate who the most persuasive and influential people are. Surely you need to know that if you want to get ahead. Let's face it; sometimes in order to get ahead, you need to know which buttons to press and how to press them so how else will you know if you ignore such factors?

84.   EARN A CERTIFICATION AND MAKE A BIG DEAL WHEN YOU DO.

If your industry has some kind of certification, get it and make it known after attaining it. There are a few examples I can think of including the Chartered Accountant, the Chartered Marketer, the Master Human Resource Practitioner or the Certified Speaking Professional. These tell people that you are on top of your game so if there's one available in your industry, be sure to acquire it and make it known once you do.

85. IF YOU ARE DISSATISFIED WITH YOUR JOB, DO SOMETHING ABOUT IT

According to a 2012 Harvard Business Review, successful and rising stars in management are also dissatisfied with their career growth. Calm down, you are not alone. "Young high achievers — 30 years old on average, with strong academic records, degrees from elite institutions and international internship experience are antsy. Three-quarters sent out résumés, contacted search firms, and interviewed for jobs at least once a year during their first employment stint. Nearly 95% regularly engaged in related activities such as updating résumés and seeking information on prospective employers. They left their companies, on average, after 28 months." (Source: Why Top Young Managers are in a Non-stop Job Hunt)

If you are dissatisfied, do something – it's in your hands.

86. USE SOCIAL MEDIA PRODUCTIVELY

A few months ago, I read a book titled 'To Quote Myself: A Memoir' by Khaya Dlanga, who is now the Senior Content Excellence and Digital at Coca Cola. I find it very fascinating how Khaya used social media to create a profile, be hired at some leading advertising agencies and eventually become so senior at Coca Cola.

Khaya couldn't finish his diploma in Advertising due to financial constraints. Instead of walloping in self-pity, he dispersed his ideas on the Internet, firstly on YouTube and then Twitter and look where he is now. Here's a summary of his profile now:

He has been awarded more than 15 advertising awards including Loeries, a Gold Cannes Lion, a Black Eagle and honorary membership in the University of the Witwatersrand Chapter's Golden Key Award. His YouTube videos have been viewed more than 6.5 million times and he has more than 12 000 subscribers to his channel, putting him in the top 5% of most viewed and subscribed users in the world.

More than 240,000 people follow Khaya on Twitter (@khayadlanga) and he was named 'Africa's top blogger' by the Highway Africa Conference. He was named in Jeremy Maggs' book, Annual 2008 on Advertising, Media and Marketing as one of the '100 most influential people in media' and was 2009 Financial Mails' Ad Focus New Broom of the Year. (Source: capebod.org.za)

If you still think social media is just for 'social' then you are terribly mistaken because social media can be a very powerful tool to springboard your career – use it wisely.

87. GET THOSE RECOGNITION AWARDS

Whether it is the South African Music Awards, the South African Women in Science Awards or any awards in your industry or organisation, if you are eligible, enter them. Recognition makes you look good on paper and puts you on the spotlight. The last time I checked, looking good on paper and being on the spotlight for the right reasons puts one in a very good position for career progression so why not?

88. NEVER EVER DEPEND ON SALARY ALONE

I think these days it is totally impractical to expect one employer to meet all your financial needs, it just doesn't work well anymore. You have to find ways to supplement your income. Many people have left jobs they really loved due to financial pressure.

> *"If your salary is the only source of income you have; you are bewitched. The person who pays your salary determines where you can stay, which schools your child can attend etc. That is total manipulation and control. It is witchcraft to live only by salary; we need multiple streams of income."*
> **Dr Bernard Nwaka.**

Globally, we have what is called 'the gig economy' where people work for many employers simultaneously. Personally, I believe this is the future. In South Africa, this is still very low compared to countries such as the United States but it will come. In the meantime though, sell Tupperware, sell Avon, shoes, and bags, do music part-time, open a retail shop and ask your son to work there, just do something.

You must however remember to chat to your manager and the risk & compliance department to determine what is allowed in your organisation before you do it.

89. KNOW YOUR VALUE

When I started speaking, I was always asked to speak for free. It was important then but I had to learn very quickly that people would not hesitate to exploit you if you don't know your value. They will say to you, "come and sing for free because so and so will be there and he might book."

In Corporate, this is evidenced by the fact that most prospective accept the first job offer they get because they are desperate to get the job. In most cases, the prospective employer was willing to revise the offer if they had just asked. Know the value that you deliver my friend.

They will try to use the "he's so humble" line to try and exploit your gift. It's a trap - don't fall for it. Those who are used to dealing with arrogant drama queens and kings struggle understanding those with a bit of humility. They mistake it for naivety and stupidity.

90. DON'T LET A PERFORMANCE-RATING STAND IN THE WAY OF YOUR DEVELOPMENT

My standpoint on performance-ratings is simple, I strongly believe and advocate for separate sessions for the performance-rating conversation and the development discussion. This is because in South Africa and many parts of the world, your performance score is linked to your increase, bonus and even career advancement opportunities. Because of this, a performance score becomes a huge determining factor and thus people fight very hard to get a good score.

In pursuit of a good score and the rewards thereof, honest developmental feedback is hindered, as you may not be receptive to it. For this reason, I believe it's best to schedule a one-on-one meeting with your manager where you focus on development outside of the normal performance cycle. In this way, you will be more open to feedback.

91. DON'T WORK FOR ONE ORGANISATION FOREVER

There was a time when this was celebrated but times have changed and some prospective employers now frown upon this. Working for one organisation for a few years is great but once you stay too long, recruiters and potential employers wonder if you are still agile enough to adjust to a new environment. Don't disadvantage yourself in this regard.

In this day and age, you need to move with the times in order to keep up so don't stay in one organisation as though you are a lizard trapped on a slippery surface, no matter how hard the lizard tries, it fails to crossover and thus requires physical removal. Likewise, if you stay too long, it will be the only place you know and you will only be forcefully removed, which in this case may mean death, retrenchment or retirement.

92. QUANTIFY YOUR CONTRIBUTION IN THE ORGANISATION

Many people, if asked, would not be able to explain clearly what their contribution to the organisation is. To address this, Human Performance Technologists recommend the significance of quantifying and documenting. Ever gone to that annual performance review discussion and relied on the fact that your manager knows what you have done? Well, that's not enough. You should be able to communicate, in output form, why you deserve a particular rating. Document and quantify.

As early as 1977, Fred Nickols had observed that, "Behaviour is individual activity whereas the outcomes of behaviour are the ways in which the behaving individual's environment is somehow different as a result of his or her behaviour." This is the sort of outcome your employer is interested in.

In order to put this to practice, you need to adopt this mentality: performance is the outcome of your behaviour; it is not your behaviour itself. Therefore, focus on the outcome. Nobody cares what you've been doing, we care about how what you've doing has impacted the organisation

Therefore, avoid general statements and focus on specifics, i.e. numbers/quantifiable results. For example, you can explain that as a security guard, you have reduced shrinkage by 22% year on year and that translates to a R4 million saving for the organisation.

93. ELIMINATE THE VARIABLES THAT MAY AFFECT YOUR JOB PERFORMANCE

In as much as I'm an advocate of accountability and 'not blaming the system', the fact is that sometimes there are other factors that may affect your performance. The HP Technologists suggest a model you can use to eliminate these. You have to make sure all these are taken care of in order to perform. These variables are:

a)   PERFORMANCE SPECIFICATIONS:

- Do performance standards exist?
- Do you know the desired output and performance standard?
- Do you consider the standard attainable?

b)   TASK INTERFERENCE

- Can your tasks be done without interference from other tasks?
- Are the job procedures and workflow logical?
- Are adequate resources available for you to perform (time, tools, staff, information)?

c)   CONSEQUENCES

- Are consequences aligned to support desired performance?

d)   FEEDBACK

- Do you receive feedback regarding your performance?
- Is the feedback you receive:
  - Relevant?
  - Accurate?

○   Timely?

○   Specific?

○   Constructive?

○   Easy to understand?

e)   KNOWLEDGE/SKILL

- Do you have the necessary skills to perform your role?

- Do you know why the desired performance is important?

f)   INDIVIDUAL CAPACITY

- Are you physically, mentally and emotionally able to perform?

(Source: The Rummler-Brache Group)

If any of these variables are not taken care of, it will be difficult for you to be the exceptional performer you can be and thus hinder your progress.

94. GET INTO THE HABIT OF ANALYSING THE BIGGEST PROBLEMS IN YOUR ORGANISATION AND ATTEMPT TO SOLVE THEM

There are many tools that you could use to diagnose problems in your organisation; I however suggest this process from Richard A. Swanson (1996):

a)   Articulate initial purpose – What is the issue?

b)   Assess performance variables

c)   Specify performance measures

d)   Determine performance needs

e)   Construct improvement proposal

95. ACQUIRE POWER/LEARN TO INFLUENCE

Have you noticed how in every organisation, certain people just wield power and therefore get things done? They have the ability to get their project on top of that IT implementation priority list. You can complain about this or you could build and acquire some power intentionally. There are different types of power bases you can tap into but most of the current theories about power use the analysis conducted by French and Raven over 40 years ago. They identified five principle sources or basis of power:

1. COERCIVE POWER:

The first is crudest form, which uses threats and punishment to achieve its ends. These could include sanctions against suppliers, dismissals for non-co-operating staff, demonstrations etc. This source of power should be used as a last resort in my view.

2. REWARD POWER:

This refers to the use of rewards to influence people's compliance. To be effective, the rewards must be desired by the target group, e.g. financial inducements. In my experience, monetary rewards work but they have their limit.

3. LEGITIMATE POWER:

Generally known as authority and implies the power to act as well as the power over resources.

4. EXPERT POWER:

This power comes from possessing specialist knowledge and skills and is dependent on the recognition of expertise by those concerned. Credibility is vital; otherwise, no one will take any notice.

> *"Competence is a key to credibility, and credibility is the key to influencing others."*
> **John C. Maxwell**

5. REFERENT POWER:

Generally known as personal power or charisma and comes from the high regard he or she is held by others. Should this falter or wane, this form of power vanishes although it's often employed in conjunction with other sources.

96. FOCUS – THERE IS SOMETHING CALLED TOO MUCH DIVERSIFICATION

Someone recently said to me, "I speak on culture, innovation, motivation, relationships, finances, future trends, HR and safety." I wanted to say, "Oh, I see, you are a chancer" but I didn't. The fact about our human nature is that we need focus because we just can't do everything.

As mentioned earlier, to attain mastery on a single element requires so much time as it is, so where does one get the time to master so many things? It's a serious mystery really!

Trust me when I say it's better to focus your energy on one of few factors so you give yourself time to master them, in that way, you will not only achieve mastery and thereby find it easy-going and effortless to compete most tasks, you will also have time for other significant things in your life such as family and 'alone' time.

97. KNOW WHO ARE AND DO YOU

Any career development is preceded by a deep search of who you are and the skills you actually have. There are a number of great career development assessment tools and models but they are basically about answering the following questions:

- What am I passionate about?
- What is the deepest aspiration of my heart?
- What gifts and talents flow naturally to me? The thing I do well?
- What do other people see in me? What are they praising you for?
- What thoughts, visions and dreams are impossible to put out of my mind?
- What career do I feel peace in my heart when I'm pursuing?
- What can I give my all to for the rest of my life even if I didn't get paid?

These are some of the questions that really helped me to discover my gift of speaking and training and my passion to help people develop in their careers.

98. FOCUS ON YOUR STRENGTHS NOT ON YOUR WEAKNESSES

Imagine your father giving you this type of advise, "find out what you do well and keep on doing it." That is what John Maxwell's father used to say to him. Wow! Whenever you see people who are successful in their work, they are operating in their strengths not weaknesses.

99. ALWAYS PAUSE AND THINK – DON'T BE ON A RAT RACE

Every now and then, please pause and think about the meaning of life, the definition of success and things that are very important. I often say that organisations are ruthless; if someone passes away on Thursday, they send flowers and start the recruitment process on

Monday. Let's all look after ourselves, rest and take time out with our families.

There are many definitions of success but I really love this one by John C. Maxwell, "Success is knowing your purpose in life, growing to reach your maximum potential and sowing the seeds that benefit others.

100. ACCEPT THIS FACT: YOUR CAREER PROGRESSION IS IN YOUR HANDS

It's no coincidence that in general, a work environment is an adult space so to speak. There's a reason it's not for children and that reason is simple, children lack accountability and ownership. As an adult, you are expected to have these elements, as they are necessary for you career progression. You must make it your mission to not only care but also pursue your own growth, development and career progression.

The biggest mistake you can ever make is to put your career progression on anyone else's hands. This is nobody's duty except your own. Everyone else can merely contribute to help you but nobody can do it for you, even the contributors will only do so because you require and push them to. You can't at your age expect your manager or HR to tell you what to do to get ahead nor push you into your desired position. You must instead prove and show them your desire, efforts and abilities and only then can they enable, empower and utilise your strengths.

Most of you really need to get this: there are very few things anyone can help you with as far as your career progression is concerned. There are very few opportunities anybody can hand over to you on a silver platter. There is literally no promotion that you will receive except through hard work, effort, discipline, character and loyalty. If you look at all these elements, they are factors that require you to possess and reflect so they are associated with you. Nobody can promote your like you can. Build and establish your brand, be your own motivational speaker and fight for your own advancement.

Do whatever is necessary within reason of course, to ensure that you get whatever it is you expect, want and desire from your career journey. Commit yourself to your own development, set yourself up for progress and ensure that you achieve fulfilment of your career goals.

#StagnationMustFall

REFERENCES AND FURTHER READING

Daska, L. 2014. 10 toxic people you should avoid like the plague. {Web} http://www.inc.com/lolly-daskal/10-toxic-people-you-should-avoid-like-the-plague.html

Greene, Robert, and Joost Elffers. 2000. The 48 laws of power. New York: Penguin Books.

Maxwell, J.C (2010). The complete 101 collection: what every leader needs to know. Tennessee: Thomas Nelson.

Tracy, B (2012). Earn what you're really worth: maximize your income in any market. New York: Vanguard Press.

CONTACT INFORMATION

To inquire about having Siphiwe Moyo speak at your next conference, contact:

Paradim People Solutions

Phone: +27 11 100 214

Email: Siphiwe@siphiwemoyo.co.za

CONNECT WITH SIPHIWE

Web: www.siphiwemoyo.co.za

Twitter: @siphiwemoyo

Facebook: SiphiweMoyoSpeaker

YouTube: SiphiweMoyo

FURTHER BOOKS BY SIPHIWE

How to be the Chief Executive of your own life!

Bulls and Bears reveal some interesting and practical life lessons learned from observing the markets. This book will inspire and drive you to be the person you are destined to be. Bulls and Bears reveal some interesting and practical life lessons learned from observing the markets. This book will inspire and drive you to be the person you are destined to be.

Some of the lessons:
All trends eventually end. If you are going through a "personal recession" be comforted: this too shall pass. You can get back up again – a lesson from the rand. Bull markets always last longer than bear markets – be bullish On the other hand – a lesson from the Economists: lesson about counting your blessings In the markets, just like in life, nobody cares how good you used to be Let the analysts talk – you are the Chief Executive.

www.ingramcontent.com/pod-product-compliance
Lightning Source LLC
Chambersburg PA
CBHW051916170526
45168CB00001B/412